MUSIC IS OUR MEDICINE

MUSIC IS OUR MEDICINE

THE STORY OF RECOVERY UNPLUGGED®

PAUL PELLINGER

LIONCREST
PUBLISHING

MUSIC IS OUR MEDICINE

The Story of Recovery Unplugged®

ISBN   978-1-61961-483-3 *Paperback*
       978-1-61961-484-0 *Ebook*

CONTENTS

INTRODUCTION

THE JOURNEY TO RECOVERY STARTS HERE

If you've picked up this book, then you're looking for a solution to addiction. You don't have time for bullshit. You won't tolerate exaggerated claims. I promise you'll get neither of those things here.

In fact, I am so confident in our addiction treatment and recovery approach that I am sharing in these pages that I only have one request of you; please read at least this Introduction and first chapter. If you like what I'm writing, keep reading the rest of the chapters. If you don't, you've only invested fifteen minutes of your time. In that short period, you may be able to save your own life or the life of someone you love.

This book is born out of the reality we face today: Addiction is more dangerous and deadlier today than ever before. The number of drug overdose deaths in the United States has skyrocketed to the highest level *ever*, from 17,415 in the year 2000 to more than 52,000 today. That's a 300 percent increase, making drugs the number one cause of death for Americans under age fifty—more than automobile crashes, suicides, or murders. Deaths from one particular class of drugs, opioids (heroin, oxycodone, fentanyl, morphine), are up 439 percent over that same time period, partly because street heroin is often laced with synthetic poisons like fentanyl. We'll cover this topic in detail in Chapter 6. The net result is that every time an addict shoots up, it could be his or her last day on earth.

The stakes have never been higher.

It's time to seek out addiction treatment that works and gets lasting results. At Recovery Unplugged, an addiction care organization blazing a trail in the treatment of chemical and alcohol dependency, we're blowing the doors off the long-accepted rehab "success rates" that have remained in the low single digits for decades. In contrast, our program produces long-term results for our clients at rates exponentially better than the standard.

You and your loved ones deserve the best possible chance

at recovery. That is what Recovery Unplugged offers, and in this book, I will show you exactly what we're doing at our rehab centers across the United States to help save lives and families.

WHEN TRADITIONAL REHAB FAILS

I have spent the last two decades collecting experiential and observational data on the traditional therapy and drug rehab world. I have witnessed it firsthand, and seen the numbers. The sad fact is that as many as 95 to 97 percent of clients relapse after completing traditional rehab programs. That translates into a pitiful 3 to 5 percent success rate.

Clearly, the old-school treatment approaches that focus on etiologies and causal factors and that communicate with the patient's head are not working. Anyone in recovery who has experienced real change and stayed clean long-term will tell you the same thing: the key to effecting long-lasting results is communicating not with the head but with the heart and soul of the client. That is precisely where Recovery Unplugged is aimed.

Our management team at Recovery Unplugged has a combined one hundred-plus years of experience in substance abuse recovery and rehabilitation. We have launched, managed, consulted, been involved in, or been clients in, literally dozens of rehab facilities that utilize all the standard therapies. Frustrated by the consistently dismal results year after year, and convinced there had to be a better way, we began developing a uniquely powerful treatment concept using music as the secret weapon.

The Recovery Unplugged program that you will learn about in the coming chapters has saved countless lives. Where other rehab and recovery centers have failed, we have succeeded by using a strategy and methods different from anything you've seen or tried before.

Recovery Unplugged is unique. Our program uses music as a powerful and highly effective therapeutic instrument to help clients recover from addiction. Recovery Unplugged operates on the premise that music is a catalyst for positive change.

Instead of traditional rehab methodologies, like throwing intellectual psychobabble up on a blackboard or trying to scare addicts straight, we envelop our clients in a musical environment that is both inclusive and empowering. They listen, analyze, compose, discuss, internalize, and most importantly, respond and discover through music that recovery is a bigger payoff than getting high.

Recovery Unplugged is not just for musicians. Most of our clients have absolutely no musical background or training of any kind. It's for people longing to get better and recover from their addictions.

MUSIC IS POWER

We know our program works. Data gathered in a collaborative study conducted in partnership with Nova Southeastern University, a prestigious Florida research institution, prove what we have known all along: that music is a powerful, motivational, transcendent tool in the fight against addiction and for long-lasting recovery. Our statistics show a groundbreaking success rate: the percentage of our clients who are staying clean twelve months posttreatment is more than four times higher than the national average. These are unprecedented results. We are changing lives with this unique therapy.

We attribute this success to a number of factors, not the least of which is that fewer clients are leaving midtreatment. More than 40 percent of clients in their twenties will typically leave traditional therapy against medical advice (AMA) before their treatment is completed. Our AMA rates are seventy-five percent better than the national average.

This is a critical difference between Recovery Unplugged

and other facilities, because the longer a person is in treatment, the better chance they have at long-term recovery. This is the first positive link in the recovery chain. If we can keep people in treatment, we have a much better shot at effecting the systemic change that is necessary. At Recovery Unplugged we have created an atmosphere conducive to positive development that deters clients from running away. We have stopped yelling at our clients, the way facilitators at many other rehab centers do, and started helping them find their inner strength.

FIGHTING AN EPIDEMIC

Everyone is finally talking about the addiction epidemic (see Chapter 6), but nobody is discussing the fact that treatment philosophies thus far have failed...miserably. In writing this book, our goal is to raise awareness not only of the problem, but also of the special Recovery Unplugged solution that we know can save countless more lives.

We are at the forefront of a revolutionary treatment movement, with facilities currently in Florida and Texas, and more locations coming soon. We've treated thousands of patients, and the data unequivocally show that our solution works. We are leading the way and changing an industry that still uses techniques from two centuries ago. In the coming chapters, you'll learn more about our unique process, how it works, why it works, and why we're on a mission to share it with the world. Our goal is, and has always been, to save as many lives from the spiral of addiction as possible. If someone you know is caught in that spiral, we can help.

If you're an addict, and you've tried and failed at rehab, the information here may literally save your life. If a loved one, family member, boyfriend, girlfriend, husband, wife, sister, brother, or anyone you care about who is an addict, this book may be the way forward...for them and for you.

If you or your loved one has tried a traditional rehab center but failed to beat addiction, we urge you keep reading and learn more about the Recovery Unplugged system. Remember our request, please read at least the first chapter. We're very proud of the work we've already done, but we know there is so much more to do. We'd love to tell you about it.

ARE YOU OR A LOVED ONE SUFFERING FROM ADDICTION? CONTACT US.

Call us 24/7 at 1-800-55-REHAB (73422)

or visit our website, RecoveryUnplugged.com.

CHAPTER ONE

THE RECOVERY UNPLUGGED® PROGRAM

The room is quiet. Guitars and musical instruments are scattered around the stage. Thirty clients are waiting for the live performance to begin. But this isn't a rehearsal hall or a concert venue.

It's a rehab facility.

The audience is made up of substance abusers and addicts from all walks of life. Their paths have intersected in rehab at an intimate, innovative treatment center called Recovery Unplugged. Though each person in the room is an individual brought to this moment by a unique set of circumstances, they are about to share an uplifting, transformational, and unifying group experience that harnesses the power of music as addiction therapy.

Legendary singer-songwriter, and Recovery Unplugged's full-time creative director, Richie Supa opens the session by telling a story.

"I was at the Florida Narcotics Anonymous annual conference, standing in the crowd on the convention center floor," he recalls. "The music was playing, and the crowd was hitting an inflatable beach ball up in the air. Every time the music stopped, the person who caught the ball had to speak. This one time, when the music stopped, a girl with one day clean caught the ball and began to speak. She said, 'I kept the right ones out and let the wrong ones in.'"

Everyone was intrigued by Richie's story.

"Immediately my songwriting antennae fly up," Richie continues. "I call Steven Tyler and say, 'Steven, man, I kept the right ones out and let the wrong ones in.' He replies, 'Yeah, I had an angel of mercy to see me through all my sins.' I say, 'Yeah, isn't that amazing?' Steven says, 'That's the name of the song! Get your ass on a plane right now.'"

Now the clients know the origin of Aerosmith's hit song

"Amazing," which shot up to number three on the charts later that year. Richie writes the lyrics on the whiteboard in front of the group. They already feel connected to its meaning. They know the backstory of one of Aerosmith's most popular ballads of all time.

Then Richie breaks out a plastic bag with a sheet of yellow paper in it. As he passes it around to the clients, they realize it contains his actual, original, handwritten lyrics. You can feel the electricity as they immediately respond. They're emoting. They're verbalizing. Most important, they're instantly engaged.

Here were a bunch of clients in rehab—the majority of whom were in their midtwenties and listened to artists like Drake and Lil' Wayne—relating to Aerosmith, a rock band that was popular before most of them were even born.

Many of these kids had been in and out of rehab facilities more times than they could count, with no lasting success. Dozens of counselors and therapists had tried and failed to reach them on a deep enough level to effect change. Yet right before their eyes, Richie spent all of three minutes framing a song and magically owned the room.

BREAKING FREE

Right now in this country the heroin epidemic, and addiction in general, has surpassed car accidents as the leading cause of death for young people under twenty-five years old. Each year we lose approximately 52,000 people to this disease. The traditional rehab system in the United States is not reducing those numbers in any meaningful way. On the contrary, the number of overdose deaths is growing every year.

Traditional treatment modalities play defense, instilling clients with a fear of the consequences if they don't do what they are told. The fact is, fear may be a temporary motivator for addicts, but it is not a deterrent. Consequences mean nothing to an addict; I'll explain why in Chapter 5. Focusing on negativity and fear will not reach the core of the issue. Unless you have rapport with these clients, it's impossible to get them to be open-minded, to change, or to alter their emotions and perceptions.

Music, on the other hand, is a universal language. Clients often have difficulty sharing what they think or feel, but I guarantee somebody's written a song that says it perfectly. If you can find the right song with the specific lyric that truly expresses what the client needs to hear or experience, you can break through to them. We've seen it happen again and again at Recovery Unplugged.

You can break down defenses that keep them from successfully moving forward. This works regardless of musical taste, artist, style, genre, or musical era. Finding that perfect song that speaks directly to a client's heart is far more effective than just asking, "So, how's your life?" or some other trite, open-ended question heard ad nauseam in rehab centers around the world.

REACHING THE ROOT PROBLEM

Drug and alcohol abuse is the symptom, not the problem. Clients are desperately seeking to fill a huge hole that is fueled by distorted perceptions, poor coping skills, a negative self-image, and the lack of a healthy support system. All of this is the perfect storm for destructive behavior. What it really comes down to is a spiritual void that can only be replaced by a spiritual entity. Some people use God, some people use meditation, some people use self-help, others use inspirational speakers like Tony Robbins or Jack Canfield.

No matter how you nourish the spirit, the one form of communication that consistently keeps clients focused, motivated, and anchored to the present is music, through both experiencing live performances and establishing positive associations. Remember how you learned the ABCs at school? It was through that simple song. No matter how many years go by, you'll never forget it. Music is the therapy that can always be with you, even after you leave treatment.

RECOVERY SOUNDTRACKS

Most treatment facilities stress avoidance of the same top five relapse triggers. Instead, we focus on positive recovery triggers that will engage clients. Consider this analogy to the childhood game Simon Says. When kids play Simon Says, if the leader says only, "Sit down," that's not a command to sit down. Key words are missing. The leader must say the indicator words first: "Simon says..." Then the children will take the command.

Music is our indicator to clients. It helps motivate them to feel grateful more than they feel unappreciated. It helps motivate them to call their sponsor when they need to. It motivates them to reach out for help, to avoid places and people that might get them into trouble. And it helps inspire them at critical moments to make the right choice. Music is the indicator because we frame it that way while they are at our facility. Music is the catalyst for change.

As part of our program, clients create soundtracks of their lives. Recorded in one of our Recovery Unplugged studios, each soundtrack is filled with songs they have chosen, witnessed others perform, or created themselves. When they leave our facility, we don't just hand them a certificate and say, "Go to meetings and don't drink." We give them an MP3 player and earbuds so they can reenter their lives with a powerful, personalized support tool. They can listen to their own personal recovery soundtrack at any time. It helps ground them when they are struggling to cope out there on their own. We'll discuss this more in Chapter 2, but let me give a quick example here.

We have a client whom I got to know pretty well. After she left Recovery Unplugged, I told her if she ever needed anything, to give me a call. Months into her recovery, she called me. She said she felt like she was getting ready to use again. But she had her MP3 player which she could use as an anchor; the music on the MP3 player would take her back to the safe place. She listened to the music, and she was able to resist the urge. But she needed more help. We brought her back into the program for a few weeks and got her back on track. Today she's doing well.

LIVING IN THE PRESENT

The therapeutic importance of being in the present cannot be overstated. If you think about where stress comes from, it's either from worrying about the future or thinking about the past. Right now, in this very second, everything's perfect, but as soon as I start focusing on the past or the future, it takes away from the present. How does one stay in the present? Many people say the key is meditation. It will train your brain to stay focused on the here and now.

However, there are other ways to be anchored to the present without using breathing techniques like meditation. Music can be that catalyst to help you stay in the present. While you are listening to a song, the more you allow yourself to surrender to it, the more present you become. The more you train your mind to stay in the present, the better you will be able to cope when life throws you a curveball out in the real world.

Recovery Unplugged strives to create a present for our clients that is warm, nurturing, and inclusive. Our supportive, encouraging environment creates a spirit of unity that helps maintain a healthy group dynamic. This is critical to therapeutic success; more will be discussed about this in Chapter 5.

TOYS FOR THE ADDICT

Recovery is a serious business, and clients can come in with an outlook that is pretty bleak. It's important to reinforce the positivity of the Recovery Unplugged atmosphere with caring and humor. Part of our job is to show clients that life without drugs can be joyful and fun. Nobody is better at that than our creative director, Richie Supa. Richie is a legitimate rock star who's toured with Aerosmith and written some of the biggest rock songs ever recorded.

One day, Richie walked into a group session with a bin full of lap drums, tambourines, and harmonicas. Alluding to a 1980s Aerosmith album titled *Toys in the Attic*, he said, "These are toys for the addict. Watch this."

He brought the instruments to the group and handed them out. As soon as he started performing a song, the clients began participating, chiming in with their instruments. When he does this with the group, they become part of the process. They feel involvement and an ownership of the facility. Instead of having the experience of somebody yelling at them or being confrontational, they are sharing a positive drum-circle experience.

Often after a group has performed, Richie will say, "Hey, look at you guys. You all look high. Wait a minute, did somebody smoke a joint in here that I didn't know about?" This is the aha moment, the payoff. They realize they are feeling high, but only from the dopamine triggered by the music; they're actually clean, sober, and feeling great without drugs. The music fires off many of the same chemicals in the brain that drugs do. At Recovery Unplugged our days are filled with moments like that.

HELP ME RHONDA

Most addiction counselors in traditional rehab facilities are trained to ask leading questions like, "So, tell me about when you were four and your uncle made you sit on his lap." It can be important to raise awareness of the past, but if that's all you've got, nine times out of ten, it just won't work. All you're doing is opening up a can of emotional worms and creating more misery in the client.

Instead, Recovery Unplugged creates a reality where clients rely on musical markers, not drugs, to guide them through the minefields they face in life. The song "I Got

This," from Richie's *Enemy* album lends itself as a perfect example of how that translates from theory into practice. The song was inspired by a Recovery Unplugged client named Rhonda.

Rhonda walked into therapy and Richie said, "How are you doing, Rhonda?" She said she was on her fifth DUI, and every time her attorney or boyfriend or parents would say "Give me the keys, Ron. Don't drink and drive," she would say, "I got this. Don't worry. I got this."

All addicts use the words "I got this" at one time or another. It's the addict's theme song. So Richie wrote the song "I Got This," a humorous, satirical look at just how ridiculous it is for an addict to think they have things under control while using or when they're in recovery. We have a sign in our group room that says, "This is where Rhonda used to sit," because Richie always explains how he created the song.

"I Got This" had such a powerful impact on one of our outpatient clients that it changed both his behavior and his mindset. One evening at around 5:30, when he was on his way home from work, he knew he needed to go to an AA meeting but was just too tired. He related to the group how he told himself, "I don't need to go to a meeting. I have two months clean. I got this." Immediately, he made the association to the song and realized how unproductive and almost funny it was for him to think, "I got this." He ended up going to a meeting that night, and he now associates that song with avoiding relapse.

That's just one example of the many opportunities music gives clients to open up a new dialogue, gain insights into their behaviors, and consider a different path.

Music is our language at Recovery Unplugged and we use it in a variety of ways to create empathy and connection. Whether we are working in groups or one-on-one, we are creating, analyzing, performing, and benefiting from music. From drum circles to open mic sessions where the clients perform, music is the primary therapeutic tool.

WATCH THE MUSIC VIDEO

You might be interested to see the music video for "I Got This," which we sponsored for recovery month, September 2017. Visit RecoveryUnplugged.com.

Please share the video with anyone who you think might be interested.

WE'RE PLAYING THEIR SONG

Every client entering Recovery Unplugged goes through a rigorous preassessment process. In traditional treatment, that process begins and ends with the clinical and financial criteria. Of course, our intake includes all of that pertinent personal and medical data, but we take it a critical step further and do a "musical evaluation" as well.

Before a client even enters treatment, we have a handle on their favorite musical genre, even narrowing it down to specific songs that have special meaning for them. Those songs may be associated with a loved one who just passed away, or their first girlfriend, or may remind them of a particularly happy time. No matter who they are or what their background, there will be a song that elicits a deeply emotional response. It never fails.

In over twenty years of interviewing addicts, I've heard it all. But there are two things I've yet to hear: "I'm a cannibal" and "I hate music." The former is proof that there isn't much our clients don't bring to the table. The latter is the reason Recovery Unplugged is so universally appropriate and effective.

Let's say you are a Beatles fan, and the song that speaks to your heart is "The Long and Winding Road." You feel the lyrics are the narrative of your life and every time you hear them, you connect to your deepest emotions. When our driver picks you up from your house, or the airport or the detox center or the hospital, and you get into our vehicle, that song—*your* song—is playing in the van. If you're not half out of it, you will immediately respond.

Our drivers have heard clients say things like, "Oh my gosh, 'The Long and Winding Road' by the Beatles. This is my favorite song. Do you like this song?" The driver will say, "Yes, and I heard you do, too." Immediately, rapport is established. The client feels heard and listened to, perhaps for the first time in years, versus having all of their past transgressions shouted in their face. Instead of rubbing their noses in the fact that they have abandoned their children, or behaved horribly to their loved ones, or whatever it is they've been repeatedly yelled at for, we find a way to immediately connect through music, which significantly eases their adjustment to rehab.

Unlike other facilities that expect a two- to three-week acclimation period for new clients, we meet them where they are, accepting them into an environment that is comforting and welcoming and musically familiar. From the moment they set foot in our van, they know they are being treated as individuals and will not be bombarded with negativity and psychobabble.

MUSICAL COLLABORATION

Much of our program is based on musical collaboration, which reinforces the sense of community. Usually we will focus on a particular topic that needs to be addressed. Let's say the topic of the day is change. A group of clients will be in a room together, and everyone will be asked to come up with a lyric specific to the subject of change. Maybe somebody will be inspired to contribute a specific hook or a chord change or a melody. Others may just write a key word on the paper. We have music studios and technical engineers on hand to handle the sound. They are so talented they can make anyone sound good—even me! That's not easy.

We all have difficulty at times putting our emotions into words, but it's easy to relate to a song that says exactly what you are feeling. Being a part of a group, and actively contributing to making music helps clients feel less threatened and more willing to open up and share.

Richie Supa and our clinicians are outstanding at getting clients to participate, regardless of age, background, or musical proclivity. They are the guides, but it is the music that compels the clients to look inside themselves and take on their inner demons. It is the music that allows them the freedom to be brave and be open to changing their behavior.

CLIENTS MAKING MUSIC

Open Mic is a wonderful opportunity for both clients and staff to perform. One of our staff members, who happens to be a professional musician in recovery, will pick up her guitar and perform a song relevant to the topic of the day. Again, if that topic is change, maybe she'll choose Michael Jackson's song "Man in the Mirror," which speaks directly to the core of the issue.

It's a lot more effective than a staff member reading from some daily reflection or daily goals book to a bunch of bored clients who drone in unison, "My goal today is to stay in the present." The words are meaningless without the spirit behind them. Hearing a song that is relevant to their story makes clients feel engaged and makes them more likely to have a heartfelt, truthful response.

"Stand by Me," written by Ben E. King, Jerry Leiber, and Mike Stoller, is also a meaningful song that we sometimes suggest to clients. There are a lot of songs with meaningful lyrics that will trigger emotional responses. More often than not, once clients feel free to really be themselves, they will come up with their own original material—even if they are not the least bit musically inclined.

Often a client who has never sung a note in public will feel compelled to stand up and share. I witnessed what can only be called a defining moment when a young woman who had only been with us a couple weeks broke out of her shell and performed. She had been severely abused—sexually, verbally, and physically—and was timid to the point of being almost completely withdrawn. We put her on a team with some other clients and asked her to practice with them and participate in creating some lyrics. Her response was negative and she kept saying, "Listen, I've never done this before, and I won't be very good."

Encouraged by her peers saying, "We love you. Just do it. You'll be fine," she actually got up and performed. You could just see the freedom and relief overwhelm her when it was over. It was as if somebody had lifted a thousand-pound weight off her shoulders. There wasn't a dry eye in the house.

That kind of breakthrough magic happens daily at Recovery Unplugged.

MUSIC EVERYWHERE

Each of our facilities is unique, warm, and welcoming, and music is incorporated anywhere and everywhere possible. For example, in our Fort Lauderdale treatment center, our clients live about a mile from the treatment facility in villas close to the beach. As they are driven back and forth, up and down Highway A1A along the ocean, a playlist is always playing.

Music can be heard in the hallways and courtyards and offices and meeting rooms throughout each of our facilities. It really works to set the tone for therapy, and also keeps the musical connection going even when clients are not actually in session. We play a loop of about three hundred songs from a wide range of genres, including music from the past and present, from Gladys Knight and the Pips to current artists like Drake, and everything in between.

For clients who don't feel like singing but are looking for a way to share, we have a professional comedian on our staff. He doubles as an improv coach for anybody who would rather tell jokes than sing. After music, laughter is the best medicine, and it helps clients see humor in their very serious situations.

THEY'VE GOT RHYTHM

Our drumming circles are a perfect combination of the physical and spiritual. Working the drums gets the blood flowing and helps release anger and negative energy while increasing endorphin and serotonin levels. As the rhythm and the vibration reaches clients on a subconscious level, their spirit is uplifted, and they become more open to positive thinking. This can be compared to experimental therapies in the 1970s and 1980s in which people used sticks to bang out their frustrations by hitting furniture or walls. Instead of beating up the couch with a bat to purge destructive thoughts, we are banging on drums in rhythm. Many studies have proven that our ability to handle stress is in direct proportion to how much we exert ourselves physically.

Often we will get a client who just sits in the circle with their arms folded, refusing to participate. They are only in therapy because a wife or family member insisted. Our staff is skilled at spotting resisters.

On the day Richie Supa brought in the "toys for the addict," among the percussion instruments in the box was one of those eggs that make a clicking noise.

He said to a client who was looking particularly disconnected that day, "Hey, can you just do me a favor and hold this while I'm playing the songs?"

The client responded, "Oh, yeah, whatever."

Richie very pointedly said, "Well, listen, man. Don't move it while I'm playing, because if you move it, it will make noise."

When Richie started playing the song, instinctively the client started shaking the egg to the beat. Before the client even knew what was happening, he was involved in the music. It works every time.

Whether clients are banging the drum, shaking the egg, or playing the tambourine, the key is to get them to become active participants in the process of making music. Instead of listening to a counselor lecture them over and over again, clients find their voice as a group through the rhythm, the lyrics, and the music.

SUCCESS STORIES

To really understand what it takes to break through and reach our clients, you have to understand how completely down and out they are by the time they get here. They've screwed up, messed up, and wasted golden opportunities. They've usually been through rehab before, and failed.

Take one young man who was picked out of literally thousands of entrants and actually made it to the stage on the NBC TV show *The Voice*. For an aspiring musician, it was the dream of a lifetime that could have set him on the track to becoming a rock star. The day before he was scheduled to appear on the show, he got high and never showed up.

Who knows whether he would have won, but can you even imagine the low esteem level he brought into therapy? He was beyond depressed and said he was totally done with music, forever. He refused to even pick up a guitar in front of the group.

During an individual session, a therapist said to him, "Do me a favor, man. Just bring your guitar in here. Just put it down and leave it there. You don't have to play it." By encouraging baby steps, she managed to convince this young man to play in the individual session.

When he started to play, it was a true transformation. The counselor watched this kid light up from the music. It was so incredible to see him regain his passion and his confidence enough that he started performing again. Now he's back on his musical path.

The story is the same, no matter where clients come from—or how old they are. A famous rock star in his late sixties who came to us seeking anonymity was barely coherent when he arrived. He had been abusing alcohol and pills for so long he could barely walk and literally could not put two words together. I took a look at him standing there shaking and decided to let his own music speak to him. If I told you the lyric I recited at that moment you would immediately know who I'm talking about, so I can't mention it. I can tell you the minute I said the first half of the line, his eyes brightened and he responded with the other half. Now he's back on his musical path and using music to stay clean.

It was remarkable because he was one step above catatonia when he walked in. But the music triggered an instant response in him. A therapist could have spent all day talking at him and gotten nowhere. One line of music allowed him to tap into a very personal, emotional space. He did well at our facility because, with the exception of a few of our older clients, nobody knew him. He was able to pursue his treatment anonymously and unencumbered.

MUSIC FINDS A WAY IN

Every day at Recovery Unplugged we see proof of the transcendence of music. Forget age or specific musical tastes. The majority of our clients prefer hip-hop on their own time. But when Richie Supa performs Aerosmith songs, or his own folksy unplugged recovery songs, there isn't a soul he does not touch.

As Richie says, "Music will always find its way in; there's no defense against it. It breaks down resistance. It teaches the spiritual principles that are needed in order to stay clean."

> **"MUSIC WILL ALWAYS FIND ITS WAY IN; THERE'S NO DEFENSE AGAINST IT."**
>
> **—RICHIE SUPA**

Even though every staff member is meticulously hand-picked and plays a critical role in our program, the success of Recovery Unplugged does not depend solely on them. They are facilitators who help set the positive, artistic tone for our nonconfrontational environment. Clients don't depend on intellectual interaction with the therapists as much as they do on becoming active participants in our program. They become members of a creative community and part of a process that makes them feel involved, supported, and free to really get in touch with their feelings.

The real star of the show is the music. It allows clients to connect on a spiritual level. It fortifies their freedom, their optimism, their faith, their relief, their gratitude.

When we communicate with the soul using music, whether creating it, witnessing it, performing it, or simply experiencing it, we are manifesting love. We are reinforcing a client's ability to wear life like a loose garment and just let things roll off. That's the kind of coping skill addicts need to make it out in the world, the kind of skill they are not getting from traditional therapy models.

THE UNIVERSAL LANGUAGE

Music has a universal impact, which is what makes Recovery Unplugged so effective. The beauty of music as a therapeutic tool is its ability to connect to any client, of any age, at any stage of life.

Our philosophy is to reframe the psychology of addiction treatment and to infuse it with the magic and joy of music. We are using music's power to push past boundaries and break down the barriers that impede healing. The music empowers clients with the confidence and self-esteem they need to make their lives work without drugs.

As Recovery Unplugged gains traction in the treatment world, we are also finding support in the music world. Richie Supa is now an invaluable member of our full-time staff. A growing list of well-known musicians, also in recovery, are eager to share their stories and their music with clients as well. In the coming chapters, we'll tell you some stories that will blow your mind.

ARE YOU READY TO GET HELP?

In the Introduction to this book we asked you to just read through the first chapter. You've done that. Thank you.

If our unique program sounds like something you want to learn more about, please get in touch with us. Whether you're an addict or a loved one, we understand the emotions you're going through right now. It's a difficult decision. Which is all the more reason to call. If nothing else, we'll lend a sympathetic ear. Or perhaps we'll help you change a life.

Our twenty-four-hour number is 1-800-55-REHAB (73422).

Another easy way to learn more about the Recovery Unplugged program is by visiting our website. Just go to RecoveryUnplugged.com. There's a lot of great information on the website, as well as some videos that allow you to see the musical performances we've talked about in this chapter. Also search us on YouTube for more videos.

If you're not ready to pick up the phone or visit our website, that's okay. We understand. How about this...while you decide what's next, why not keep reading this book? There's a lot more helpful information in the remaining chapters. We'll dig in to how music affects the human brain, our clients and results, addiction in America, the history of drug rehab, and a whole lot more. By the end of this book you'll be well-informed and able to make the right decision for yourself.

You'll also see some sidebars titled "Clinician Q&A." These are interviews with some of our staff members who work with clients every day. I think you'll find their perspective not only interesting, but also relevant to your decision about whether or not to look deeper into the Recovery Unplugged program. At the very least, they'll probably answer some of the questions floating through your mind right now.

CLINICIAN Q&A WITH IAN JACKSON, CLINICAL DIRECTOR, RECOVERY UNPLUGGED®

LICENSED MENTAL HEALTH COUNSELOR

Is the response to music hardwired into all humans?
There is a lot of science that shows how the human brain responds to music in a similar way to how it responds to drugs. Rhythm is ingrained into people's bodies and into people's souls. If you put on a song almost anywhere you go, a song that people dance to, or a song you play at a wedding, somebody is going to be bopping their head. We just truly believe in what music can do for people in recovery. It's a very scary thing to come into treatment, and when you feel a little more comfortable and you feel at home and you have that safety, it makes things a little easier.

What's different about the admission process at Recovery Unplugged®?
When a client calls up for help, we put them through an admission process similar to other treatment centers, with some exceptions. We ask them a series of questions, including what their favorite genre of music is and their favorite bands. That way, when we pick up that client from the airport, we're going to have that music playing in our van, which helps create rapport with them. It's a subtle way of letting them know we're listening. A lot of our clients might not be musically inclined, but everybody has a favorite song.

Everybody has instances in their life where they use music to feel more comfortable. When the client is admitted to our treatment center, we have an MP3 player for them. Each MP3 player has about ten gigs of music loaded onto it, all sorts of music from Bob Marley to the Beatles.

What happens next?
One of the first groups that they attend when they come to Recovery Unplugged is called the Songs of Life. In the Songs of Life group, we actually have a form that they will fill out with one of our facilitators that identifies songs that are meaningful to their life. These could be songs that they listened to when they were kids or songs that make them happy or songs that give them energy or songs that they listen to on a rainy day or songs that they would listen to if they were celebrating something. We want to identify these triggering songs that inspire them to live a better life.

There are times when I see a client in a pretty upset mood, and I know that client is about to come into my group. I'll go look through their chart real quick. I'll pick out a song that makes them happy, or a song that inspires them. I'll start the group with that song. Nine times out of ten, that client is going to be the first one to share by saying, "Oh wow, I love that song. I used to listen to that all the time." Or "I used to listen to that song when I was really upset. That's my pump-up song." What we do is use music as a catalyst to engage clients in treatment.

Can you learn a lot about a client just by the music they like?
Definitely. When I'm downloading music for a client and they give me a list of songs, it's almost like I can tell their

life story by the songs they want on their MP3 player. I can see the songs that they used to listen to before they battled addiction, and then I can see songs that they're listening to now that they are trying to get clean. There's a big difference. There are the songs they have been listening to recently, in active addiction, which may be a little more provocative, or they may be a little more indicative of those behaviors.

What's the idea behind the MP3 players?
There are therapeutic advantages to using music as a way for clients to associate and retain the information they learned while at Recovery Unplugged. We want to help our clients take treatment home with them through music. When they're having a rough day and they really want to get motivated, they play that song about perseverance, and they're going to remember what was said in that group. They're going to remember that conversation. They're going to play that song that will bring back memories immediately.

We spend a lot of time transitioning a client onto the next level of care, whether that be home or sober living and continued outpatient therapy. In the transition period, silence can often be a client's worst enemy. They can get up in their own head and start spinning around. Being able to have a client take that MP3 player home with them and be able to listen to those songs at night, or when they feel stressed, is so powerful. I get clients that tell me they listen to the same song every morning; it's their wake-up song. They put the same song on every night when they're about to go to bed. That is what we are trying to do, to identify recovery triggers. We want them to seek those experiences. Rather than avoiding pain, avoiding anxiety, avoiding grief, and avoiding loss, we want them to seek healing.

Are the clients or their families ever skeptical of using music for recovery?

I have never had a family question what we do. The family members of clients who are musically inclined are in love with the place. They say things like, "I just feel like this is such a godsend because of the approach and the music. I just know it's helping him so much."

Take a family member of a client who has no music inclination. When I have that first call with that parent, which is usually in the first couple of days of the client being here, I explain to them what we do and why we use music. I also encourage them to check out our website. I ask them to watch a couple of the videos and read the testimonials because I want them to understand. I explain to them how we use music as a catalyst.

How does music foster communication between clients and their families?

Music is a magnificent tool for treatment because it can help a client understand how their family members feel, as well as let the family members understand how the client feels.

I had a client recently tell me, "My family just doesn't understand me. They don't understand why I use drugs. They don't get why I just can't stop using." He had this song that he said perfectly explained how he felt and why he uses.

I said, "I'm going to take this song, and with your permission, I am going to send it to your family. I am going to ask them to listen to it with the lyrics."

There was a night and day difference between his family members' attitude before that and their attitude on the next phone call I had with them after they listened to that song. They were in tears.

They said, "We didn't understand how he was feeling or how he was affected."

People can communicate through music. When someone gets married and they choose their wedding song, they associate that song with love and connection. Just as a song can be associated with love and connection, it can be associated with pain and loss, or grief, or disappointment.

Is it difficult for new clients to adjust to the Recovery Unplugged® program?
When we take the drugs and alcohol away from clients who are addicts, they often become very inhibited because most addicts suffer from poor self-image and low self-esteem. By encouraging them to create and participate in the therapeutic process, music becomes the catalyst for cognitive behavioral therapy, which is a two-dollar way of saying it changes their thinking and behaviors.

Most treatment centers only focus on the clients' thinking and their feelings. Very few treatment centers engage them in the action or the behavior change that's necessary. Having the clients participate and get up in front of a bunch of strangers and recite poetry or perform music or dance helps them practice what they're going to need to do when they get out of treatment. Because they've done it in a safe environment, it is easier for them to do it when they leave.

Can you think of an example of somebody who came in who was scared or uneasy and how the music helped them?
I had a client recently who was twenty-six years old and had been using crystal meth for a long time. He had been to several treatment centers and he had a lot of anxiety about being in treatment. He always felt like he was trapped and enclosed, and he never truly felt comfortable with the other people in the facility.

When he first came in, he identified a lot of music that he liked. When he was talking about those songs, he started to get a little more comfortable.

I asked, "Do you play a musical instrument?"

He said, "Well, kind of. I was a drummer for ten years, but I honestly haven't even touched a drum kit in years and I haven't taken my drum kit out of my closet in five years."

We have a drum set at Recovery Unplugged, so I handed him the drumsticks, and I said, "I want you to just get up there and mess around a little bit."

He was an incredible drummer! After he began to play, his whole persona changed. Next thing you know, he's playing drums during break, during lunch, and during the Open Mic group. He was drumming for people when they were playing music. He would do solos. He would read poetry and drum on the side.

He said, "Ian, I just regained my passion. I forgot what my passion was, and my passion has always been music and drumming and producing music and making music." He used to mix and edit and record music. He said, "I have been looking for something for five years, and it was music. I knew something was missing from my life, and it was the music. Now that I think back on it, in the last five years, I honestly don't even remember the last time I put on my headphones."

This revelation changed his whole persona, and he became so much more outgoing. Prior to this, he was an AMA risk, which is someone who leaves treatment against medical advice. He had left treatment against medical advice from about eight or nine other facilities in the last three years before coming to us.

What's the best part of your job?
I am passionate about what I do personally, and I'm grateful to be a part of Recovery Unplugged. The most amazing part of my job that I am extremely grateful for is the ability to watch miracles happen every day. There are people dying every day in our country and across the world right now due to drug abuse and addiction. By working at Recovery Unplugged, I get to see change every day. There is never a boring day when I go to work. Every single day is different, and I get to watch people grow and change for the better. We are in the business of second chances. I love watching people grow and recover, and then seeing the effect it has on their loved ones.

We help the families heal, too, because this is a family disease. The family goes through as much pain as the client does.

We get calls from families six months or a year later saying, "Oh my gosh, you saved my daughter's life, as well as our family."

I always say to them, "Listen, your daughter or son saved his or her own life with our guidance."

What is the Recovery Unplugged® facility like?
The facility is great. We have a stage with high-class sound, lighting, recording and editing capabilities, guitars, bass, drums, bongos—anything you can think of. The facility is a warm environment. It's a high-energy atmosphere. It's so far from being a hospital. We don't want the client to feel institutionalized while they're here. Everything from the songs they hear in the van when they come in to the kind of light bulbs that we put in our ceiling, we are thinking about making this atmosphere comfortable for our clients.

In our group rooms we have music memorabilia. One of our group rooms has posters on the wall of musicians who have actually passed away from drug and alcohol addiction. We have another group room that has posters of musicians who are in recovery, which can be inspiring. A lot of times the clients say, "Wow, that was such a great talent, and this person had everything they ever wanted, but they still died of this disease." The other thing they say is, "Wow this artist has everything they ever wanted, and they have the ability to use all the drugs they want with unlimited money, yet they're choosing not to because they want to live a better life."

What are "Feel Good Fridays"?
The Feel Good Friday group is the last session every Friday. That's when Richie and a couple of other staff members, as well as guest musicians, some legendary, come in and perform live music. Richie plays songs from his album *Enemy*, plays some covers, and even takes requests from the clients. The energy in there is amazing. They've got the lights going. The clients are jumping up and down. Some of the songs that have a synchronized dance beat will get everyone up on their feet. It's amazing. Once when a group was leaving after a session, I remember a client who said, "When I was sitting on the bathroom floor last week with a needle in my arm, I would never have believed that I would be jumping up and down to music one week later."

CLIENTS AND RESULTS

Building a unique rehab center based on a radically different treatment philosophy has drawn plenty of skepticism. It's not as if the treatment community was rallying to our cause or embracing our ideas. At least not at first.

When they heard that Recovery Unplugged was offering music-centric treatment for addiction, they weren't exactly making fun of it, but close to it. We heard comments like, "So let me get this straight. I have a client who is smoking crack, and he's going to get clean by listening to somebody play the guitar?"

We understand the skepticism. It's human nature. Throughout history, the entrenched establishment has always resisted new ideas and new ways of doing things—even when it's a better way. Recall how the hundred-year-old taxi cab industry fought tooth and nail to resist ridesharing companies Uber and Lyft. In the end, the better solution prevailed. Addiction treatment is a multibillion-dollar industry that is set in its ways. (You'll learn the history of rehab in Chapter 7.) We knew that in order to earn respect, the proof would have to be in our results.

CONVINCING OUR CRITICS

As the kids say, "Haters gonna hate." But even in the face of that early cynicism, pessimism, and downright derision, swimming upstream against the current of insurance companies and existing medical and evidence-based models, we persisted. We felt sure that if we presented a superior quality product, it would prove itself.

We started inviting small groups of guests to sit in and observe the magic up close and personally. Their response was phenomenal. In a very short time, we were changing their hearts and minds. Our guests would say, "I understood the Recovery Unplugged program intellectually, but until I saw it for myself, I didn't really get it. Now I do."

And that was only the beginning. Recovery Unplugged caught on locally and moved into the national spotlight when Steven Tyler made an appearance at our facility in Fort Lauderdale. Even the fiercest detractors have begun to change their tune, acknowledging our program as innovative, unique, and best of all, effective.

We knew the rehab system was broken, and it was. As Sam Cooke sang, "A Change Is Gonna Come." Change did come. The results are in. We are changing the face—and voice—of addiction therapy.

THE METRICS

As I mentioned briefly in the Introduction to this book, traditional rehab facilities across the industry have seen a discouraging posttreatment relapse rate of upwards of 95 percent within the first year. That's only a 5 percent success rate. It can hardly be called success. But it's an accepted outcome in the industry.

Recovery Unplugged is crushing that statistic.

Our success rate is more than four times higher than the national average, according to recent national studies. In fact, at the time of this writing, Recovery Unplugged has treated more than one thousand clients. More than four hundred of our clients, ranging from three months to over three years posttreatment, are still clean. This is clinical proof that in aiming at the heart instead of the head we are hitting the bull's-eye.

We realized we were onto something from the very beginning. You know you are doing something right when kids who normally bolt against medical advice (AMA) are sticking it out for the entire length of treatment. At traditional treatment facilities, there is often one full-time employee whose job is just to deal with the 42 percent of clients who want to leave midtreatment. Recovery Unplugged does not have that staff position.

Soon after we opened, we noticed that clients were not leaving the program. As a matter of fact, the opposite was true. We were having to tell clients, "All right dude, you've been here three months. It's time to leave." Only about 7 percent of our clients are leaving treatment AMA, which is unheard of in the rehab field. That means 93 percent of our clients are completing the program. In my more than two decades of working with treatment facilities, none has ever even come close that figure. It is both startling and humbling.

This AMA statistic alone should put Recovery Unplugged at the top of anyone's list.

Our metrics are exciting and promising, but we are going

a step further to establish our credibility. We are collaborating with the Nova Southeastern University Psychology Department, allowing their research staff access to our clients in order to compile long-term statistical data. Our goal is an objective, evidence-based model. So far, the research is backing up our own findings.

POSITIVE PERFORMANCE

The consensus from the 93 percent of our clients who complete treatment is shock and amazement—in a good way—at their progress. No matter the strength of their intellectual and physical opposition, they find they are unable to resist music's visceral effects. The impact is profound and lasting.

Many clients have been to multiple treatment centers and expected the same old, same old. It doesn't take them long to realize we don't just say we are different. We are different. Clients leave Recovery Unplugged surprised and grateful, asking what the hell just happened?

One of the things I've always found perplexing is the way most other treatment centers hire their staff. It completely ignores one of the biggest attributes that most addicts in recovery have: they have street smarts and intuition. But most treatment facilities hire their staff based almost entirely on their experience, professional credentials, and the letters behind their name. Those things are important, of course, but in my opinion, what is equally important is hiring staff based on their passion, and based on our gut feelings about each applicant during the interview process.

We like to hire staff who treat recovery as a mission rather than just a job. This is reflected in the culture we've created in our Recovery Unplugged facilities. And I believe it's why our clients give our staff a ninety-plus percent positive approval rating in our exit interview survey. That's way higher than the typical fifty-five percent staff approval rating in the more than thirty treatment centers I've been affiliated with in the last twenty years.

Through teamwork and consultation, we are constantly fine-tuning our approach, learning what to discard, and reexamining what is working to make it even more effective. Unhampered by the parameters of existing rules or guidelines, our team is charting new territory as we carve out and hone our unique curriculum.

More and more data is confirming that clients are hearing our song. They are leaving the confines of the facility, but armed with their personalized soundtracks and their new relationship with music, they are holding fast to the ideals of the program, keeping the recovery momentum going and staying clean. The proof is in our alumni-based clientele, or lack thereof. Typically, some thirty percent of clients at most rehab facilities come from the pool of relapsed returnees. Our client alumni population is less than five percent because our graduates are not relapsing.

With results like these, even the staunchest of skeptics are acknowledging our program is working. Lawyers, judges, and other criminal justice professionals who had been referring clients to us are becoming clients themselves when they or their family members have DUIs or legal or clinical issues. Owners of other facilities aren't just sending us their clients, they are sending us their loved ones. There is no higher level of trust than referring family and friends.

BREAKING DOWN BARRIERS

When people see the magic that happens at Recovery Unplugged they always ask the same question: How do you get clients who are broken, scared, beaten down, and completely closed to open up? The truth is, we don't. We could yell at them all day and night, and it would never elicit any response at all. It's the music that speaks to them. It's the music that makes its way through their shells and into their hearts.

In the same way that a particular song can transport us

through time to the backseat of a car on a favorite child-hood vacation with our parents, or make us recall our wedding day, music can help an addict heal the past while motivating them to go forward instead of backward. Music can alleviate a dangerous mood and be the difference between staying clean and sinking into the abyss.

It is that powerful.

Think about the song "What a Wonderful World," by Louis Armstrong. No matter the circumstances, that song would change the mood in the room. It's an unconscious response, so there is no defense against it. It's instinctive.

No matter how big a fight a client puts up, music will triumph. We were working with a young man who almost made it to the major league as a pitcher for the Chicago Cubs. He got injured, started using, and blew his career. He's really tight with his parents, so we asked them to send us a song that would remind him of the good times. They identified a song that was meaningful and sent it to us. He could not have been more resistant to therapy at first, but when we played that song for him, he immediately broke down. This cathartic moment was the beginning of his journey forward.

MUSIC PENETRATES

During meetings at AA or NA, many sharers spew out a lot of recycled program data that they have learned in traditional treatment centers. Though most of them have been in and out of multiple rehab programs and could recite the therapeutic litany by heart, it is not penetrating their inner core. They are only going through the motions. When they relapse, they just go back for more of the same psychobabble. The cycle remains unbroken. It's as if these individuals have forgotten how to feel.

Music can rekindle emotions that have been buried under addiction. Music penetrates. Music can release feelings that have been trapped and suppressed. Music can revive the spirit and get clients to a place of joy again. Once they get there, they see how much better life can be, and they feel that indeed recovery can be a better payoff than getting high.

Think of Bugs Bunny and the Tasmanian Devil. In order to get the Devil to calm down, Bugs would take out his violin and start playing. Immediately, the Devil would stop spinning. As Bugs would then say, albeit butchering a literary allusion, "Music calms the savage beast." We're calming the savage beast of active addiction by using music. And we are doing it in a way that is totally nonthreatening, gently breaking down defenses after changing moods and anchoring clients to the skills, perceptions, and behaviors that we're teaching them.

MUSICAL PRESCRIPTIONS MAKE IT PERSONAL

Even if our conscious selves are shut off to outside stimuli, our unconscious selves can still respond to music. For example, we've seen for years how music can benefit patients with Alzheimer's. A great example is an elderly gentleman who hadn't spoken for months; he was basically comatose. Every once in a while, the nurse would come in and play music. She noticed that when her patient heard the Cab Calloway song "Hi De Ho," he would start moving a finger on his right hand. It would bump just a little bit to the music. Over time, this spread to his whole hand and then his body. Eventually he was forming a word or two. Before they knew it, he was talking again.

As we are finding at Recovery Unplugged, carefully selected and targeted music can dramatically increase therapeutic effectiveness. We call this aspect of treatment "musical prescription."

Imagine that you tell me that you are struggling with the loneliness of recovery. Lyrics from the song "Desperado" by the Eagles can speak to that pain, especially if you are a client who is having difficulty putting your own words to it.

There is an art to finding just the right lyric to connect with a client's particular need. With a supply of songs that is virtually unlimited, if one doesn't work, another one will. Finding the song that perfectly connects to a client is one of the most rewarding parts of Recovery Unplugged.

There was a particular young man who refused to take any responsibility for his behavior. He blamed his father, his injury, and his doctor. He was not unique. Often addicts paint themselves as victims, holding everybody but themselves accountable for their situation. Instead of saying to him, "Look, we've never met any victims who recover. You need to step up and be responsible," which would have fallen on deaf ears, we used a musical prescription. We asked if he was cool with analyzing a lyric with us. He replied with the old "Yeah, whatever." We started with the song "Already Gone" by the Eagles, which addresses the idea that we have the key to unlock our personal prison and regain our freedom. That immediately got his attention.

He said, "Yeah, I get that. I understand that."

We analyzed the lyrics with him, making it personally meaningful and significant, then reinforced it by playing the song.

After working one-on-one, we played that song in the

group setting to strengthen his sense of communal support. With that song on his musical soundtrack, the next time he feels like a victim, instead of engaging in the usual negative self-talk in the mirror, he can play that song, and instantly it will be a positive recovery trigger that reminds him to let go of that victim mentality.

Another client, newly sober, was struggling with facing the reality of sexual abuse from his past, to the point of being suicidal. We began working with the Aerosmith song "Cryin'." To a nonaddict, the words in that song may appear to be about a relationship, but they are really about Steven Tyler saying goodbye to drugs. The words resonated with this young man and "Cryin'" became his go-to song. Routinely, any time he finds himself in that negative space, he will seek out a quiet place and listen to those words. It will center him and bring him peace. The negative episodes have become less and less frequent, but each time, that particular song helps him redefine the moment.

MUSICAL CONNECTIONS

A musical connection will soften even the most hardened of individuals. One of our clients was a drug dealer with prison body art and a history of violence.

He said to the group, "Yo, I ain't going to smoke no more,

but I'm definitely going to have to keep dealing. I'm in the projects, man. How else am I going to survive?"

We love these tough guys, even if they are challenging as clients. We said to him, "Hey, are you willing to meet with one of us?"

He said, "Yeah, whatever."

I started the conversation with, "Where are you from?"

He mumbled, "The Bronx."

I said, "Cool. I'm a Yankees fan."

That really didn't do it for him. He said, "Yeah, big deal, I don't care about baseball."

I persisted. "Have you ever heard of KRS-One?"

He immediately looked more interested and responded, "Yeah, he's from the Boogie Down Bronx."

"I know. He wrote a rap about how 'Love's Gonna Get'cha.'"

After we analyzed the lyrics, he realized he wasn't alone in how he was feeling.

Right away, he knew I understood where he came from, not by showing empathy or nodding or giving him a concerned "hmmm," but by throwing out a lyric he could instantly connect to. I was able to reach him through the work of a musical artist from his neck of the woods and then establish rapport with him.

He made so much progress that we put him through some vocational rehab to develop a skilled trade that would keep him from returning to dealing. He ended up staying down here in our own transitional housing instead of going back to the Bronx. Now he's over seven months clean.

OPENING MINDS

When it comes to fostering open-mindedness—which is one of the principles behind the twelve steps—music will beat traditional talk therapy every time. Here's a typical example. We had a client whose preassessment indicated that he absolutely hated country music. We saw this as a great opportunity to use music to work on improving his open-mindedness.

So in one of our group sessions, we picked a song lyric that we thought he would relate to. We didn't tell him, "Hey, we're working on open-mindedness." Instead, the group leader said, "Hey, let me put a lyric up on the screen. Maybe we can talk about it."

He didn't tell the client it was from a country song by Kenny Chesney. We knew if that client heard the actual song he would know it was a country song and resist the message. We only told him it was a song lyric, not what genre or artist it was from.

After we put up the lyric, the group leader started discussing it with the client. Those words summarized how he was feeling about himself as a man, husband, father, and provider, and they immediately sparked a conversation. The client became very engaged with the idea of what the lyric meant, and it led to a deep discussion.

Then, after discussing the lyric and its meaning, the group leader said, "Now we're going to play the song that lyric comes from."

The music began and the Kenny Chesney song played.

The client immediately said, "Oh man. I hate country music."

The group leader replied, "Yeah, we know you don't like country music, but you love the meaning of this lyric, right? What we're trying to teach you is open-mindedness. Just because you don't like that genre of music doesn't mean there aren't examples in that genre of music of how you might want to consider living your life."

We took something that was a negative for him and turned it into a positive. The client experienced what it was like to be open-minded and let something unexpected in. Sometimes in therapy, you have to take an indirect route to your goal.

We'd love to take credit for all the success stories, but we can't. It's the music that allows us to meet clients on their individual levels and create a bond that makes them comfortable enough to become part of our process. Working with specific song lyrics has done wonders for clients with whom talk therapy has already failed.

A LITTLE TRAVELING MUSIC

Most addicts lose the momentum of therapy the minute they exit a treatment facility. But for our clients, the beat goes on long after they leave the premises.

Working in our studio, clients create a soundtrack of their stay made up of songs they identify with, songs they've created, or songs they've witnessed being performed.

Each soundtrack is different, specific to the needs of each individual. Armed with the MP3 player and earbuds we give them, clients have a portable recovery catalyst they can turn to at any time, day or night. It serves to immediately transport their spirits back to treatment and to recall the thoughts, perceptions, and coping skills necessary to sustain long-term recovery.

It becomes an associative tool, an anchor that restores equilibrium and fosters gratitude, humility, and optimism. Tapping into a particular emotion or mood, the music is internalized and becomes a key element of living clean. The effect is on the soul, which is where long-lasting change occurs. Contentment and peace replace fear and anxiety, once again making sobriety a better choice than getting high.

A therapeutic tool is only as effective as the client's willingness to use it, and who can resist listening to music? It's as if somebody said eating chocolate would keep you sober. Music is our chocolate, and there are no calories involved!

It is far easier to hit play and listen to great music than it is to take out a piece of paper and pen and write in a journal every day. Soon it will be even easier, with an app to access the soundtrack on any smartphone. Wherever the music is coming from, nobody has to tell an addict, "Listen to it, or else."

CLIENT SUCCESSES

A client spoke at an NA meeting recently, sharing that she had been in and out of at least ten different treatment centers. She told the group how Recovery Unplugged worked for her because she was able to take what she had learned there to a different level, outside of treatment. She referenced the earbuds and the MP3 player. She explained that she listens to music every day, just like everyone else. But her music is a specifically tailored soundtrack designed to change her mood and get her focused on going to a meeting, calling her sponsor, or just being grateful to be sober. Her music is her personal catalyst, her lifeline outside of the treatment environment.

Another client with a wife, kids, and a sick mother did very well in treatment. Upon leaving Recovery Unplugged, as soon as his plane landed, the family bombarded him with the stress of daily living—bills, the mortgage, his boss who called wondering where he had been. The anxiety of it all threatened to derail him. He hooked up his MP3 to the Bluetooth in the car and asked his family if they would mind if he listened to some music before continuing the conversation. Bob Marley's song "Three Little Birds" filled the car, and within minutes, his mood and the mood of his entire family was altered. Not only did he feel better, but he was able to make them feel more comfortable that everything indeed was gonna be alright.

Soon the whole family was singing together in support, which bolstered his confidence in his ability to be a good husband and father. The music helped him reframe his circumstances in a gentler, more positive light. It was exactly the kind of constructive reinforcement he needed in that moment.

Statistics show that clients are the most vulnerable to relapse within the first forty-eight hours of leaving treatment. Hence, one of our catch phrases is "What was done in thirty days can be undone in thirty minutes." If they can get through that period, their odds of staying sober greatly improve. This client's soundtrack provided that extra impetus to get over the initial hump.

As both our critics and clients are learning, music can be used as an anchor to remember what was learned in treatment. Hearing a particular song or playing the soundtrack of their stay elicits a deeply spiritual response that words cannot evoke. The music will conjure up those happy, drug-free memories from the treatment environment and recreate that positive energy. Again, music is the catalyst for changing feelings and behavior. The music will trigger the desire to stay clean and to stay clear of that destructive lifestyle. It's the thread of continuity that keeps clients connected to their mission of sobriety.

WE'VE ALL GOT THE MUSIC IN US

We often get calls from other professionals saying, "Hey, we have a piano player who is a serious addict. I think he'd be great for your facility," mistakenly thinking we only treat musicians. This could not be further from the truth.

Music is our form of therapy, but we are not a niche facility for musicians. The founders of Recovery Unplugged are not musicians. Over 85 percent of our clients are not musicians. When you have a universal language that communicates directly to the heart and soul, there is no client beyond its reach. The magic of music is its ability to impact everybody. No matter where you are musically, you can't help but feel its effects and appreciate it.

Our approach is targeted at addicts of all ages, stages, lifestyles, and issues. If you can't play the piano when you arrive at Recovery Unplugged, chances are you won't be able to play when you leave. But you will gain a profound appreciation for the gift of music and a powerful ally in your fight against addiction.

Clients who have never performed or written music are empowered by participating in the musical process. We'll take a group of six clients and ask them to come up with a phrase or lyric on a certain subject. Each will say, "I've never written a song, I don't sing, and I don't know how to play an instrument." By the time they complete or perform a song with a little assistance from our staff professionals, they will have faced their fears, challenged their inhibitions, and enhanced their self-image and self-esteem. Equally as important, the exercise provides a musical outlet for emotions dulled and suppressed by years of drug use.

Music penetrates the numbness, bringing clients back to life. Literally. It not only sparks feelings that may not otherwise be expressed, but it also provides a structure for dealing with them. What looked insurmountable and overwhelming while they were using is cast in a more hopeful, positive light. It's a lot more productive than a therapist trying to pry feelings out of a closed-off client.

With traveling music conveniently available on an MP3 player, they don't need a prescription. They don't have to call anybody. They don't have to pay for it. They can never run out of it. The music is always there, and they can access it any time they need it.

The twelve steps warn that sometimes a sponsor is not going to answer the phone, and the decision of whether or not to use drugs is going to be just between you and your higher power. We've created a new scenario in which support is available anytime. All you have to do to find help is push play and your musical anchor is there.

HEALING MIND, BODY, AND SPIRIT

Clients pick up the Recovery Unplugged vibe the minute they walk through the door. Unlike other facilities that are noisy and chaotic, our ambiance is tranquil and gentle, and, dare we say, even fun. At our Fort Lauderdale location, the setting is serene and stunning, anything but institutional.

Our handpicked staff members are sensitive and passionate, and will engage clients with eye contact and smiles. Any room you enter will have music playing. It is the ideal combination of positive physical, mental, and emotional stimulation. And that is by design.

As Bill W. of Alcoholics Anonymous wrote in his book *Alcoholics Anonymous*, addiction is a physical, mental, and spiritual disease, and the solution must be aimed accordingly. At Recovery Unplugged we are providing the framework for music to reach clients on a deeper level, soothing mind, body, and soul.

As described earlier, our program integrates music into the forefront of treatment from the get-go, beginning with setting the musical tone at the preassessment. We target individual therapy with personalized music selections, finding clarity through lyric analysis. We replace the traditional goals group with Mic Check. We have performances that promote the topic of the day. We support clients in their creation of original songs that are healing and cathartic. We use music globally, both on its own and in conjunction with other therapies to enhance their impact. Music is always center stage.

ALTERED PERSPECTIVES

With a change of environment and a healthier mental space, breaking down and analyzing lyrics can completely alter the way a client relates to familiar music. With a new context, songs once associated with despair and getting high can be reframed into meaningful recovery anthems.

Take Pink Floyd's "Comfortably Numb," a popular song to get high by. When you examine the message they were trying to convey, I believe the song is really about the dangers of shooting up. There are lyrics throughout the song that reinforce the dangers and consequences of using heroin. Hearing those words in a state of sobriety paints a picture for addicts of where they have been and where they never want to go again. After analysis, their perspective is totally different.

By the time clients leave Recovery Unplugged, they may have completely overhauled their musical tastes. They may come in listening to music that is dark and depressing, a reflection of where they are emotionally, and leave with songs that are more upbeat and optimistic. If you're still listening to songs that glorify pimps, hoes, drugs, or sexual abuse, that can be a gauge of where you are in terms of recovery.

If I'm in a bad frame of mind and I'm driving down I-95 and somebody cuts me off, I might get angry, give him the finger, or even chase him down. If I'm spiritually fit, I will give him the benefit of the doubt. Maybe he's in a rush. His child could be in the hospital. In other words, that's a good gauge of where I am in my recovery. Musical tastes can provide the same barometer.

MUSICALLY ENHANCING TRADITIONAL MODALITIES

Though music is our continuous guiding light, we do not completely jettison every tool from traditional therapy. Cognitive behavioral therapy, rational emotive therapy, motivational interviewing, psychiatry, and psychology are part of our treatment program. By integrating them into our musical model, we enhance the effects of these existing modalities, allowing us to offer the best of all treatment worlds.

For example, in our version of cognitive behavioral therapy

(CBT), instead of verbally trying to alter a client's behavior, we use songs as a trigger.

A New York client says, "Every time I drive over the George Washington Bridge, I feel like getting high because it leads right to Harlem."

Normally, a cognitive behavioral approach would be, "Well, think about taking the Tappan Zee Bridge."

Maybe for some clients, it is that simple. But what if I were to designate a song as the trigger to take the Tappan Zee? Hearing David Bowie sing the song "Changes" could be used to motivate that positive response. That song would then become the catalyst for the CBT.

Rational emotive therapy (RET) is a two-dollar way of saying, "If you think about your decision and play the scenario all the way through to its conclusion, what will the consequences be?" Suppose the client is looking for freedom but with all the demands of life or the boss or the boyfriend, it is elusive. Mistakenly, that client has always abused drugs to find freedom. RET would ask that client to consider all the consequences before acting.

RET, Recovery Unplugged style, would use a lyric from the Janis Joplin song "Me and Bobby McGee," which talks about freedom and the cost of losing it. That song could then be used as a catalyst to remind clients to think through the potential consequences of their actions.

In the same way that we are using music to complement the effectiveness of the basic principles of therapy, we are also strengthening the power of NA and AA. Music doesn't have to be in a good mood during therapy. Its effectiveness does not hinge on the appropriate experience or skill set. Music is the sponsor that is available 24/7 to support and inspire clients to stay on the path and go to a meeting. Music takes the unreliable human variable out of the twelve-step equation, exchanging it for a more dependable entity that always performs. It is the sustenance that clients can always reach for to remind them to stay focused on recovery.

Music is the universal truth that sparks an immediate association with recovery and adherence to the Steps. It works as an assistant to the Steps, generating almost a Pavlovian response.

IT FEELS GOOD

Recovery Unplugged was born of a pure desire to take advantage of the power of music to help people. It's about healing the soul.

Well aware that most clients are coerced against their will into rehab by friends and family, we knew that music would reach even the most resistant clients in spite of themselves. It has that effect on most people. We want a stay at Recovery Unplugged to have the same impact: to be more of an experiential transformation than a stint in rehab.

And now, here we are, definitively changing the lives of addicts, providing them with the skill, tools, and motivation to stay clean.

ARE YOU OR A LOVED ONE SUFFERING FROM ADDICTION? CONTACT US.

Call us 24/7 at 1-800-55-REHAB (73422)

or visit our website, RecoveryUnplugged.com.

CLINICIAN Q&A WITH CHERYL EMERY, PRIMARY THERAPIST, RECOVERY UNPLUGGED®

MASTER OF SCIENCE IN PROFESSIONAL COUNSELING,
REGISTERED MENTAL HEALTH COUNSELOR INTERN,
CERTIFIED ADDICTION PROFESSIONAL

Can you walk me through a typical day at Recovery Unplugged®?

You can change your state of mind and energy level with physical activity. Every morning, right when the clients get here we have a Pump-up group session. It's the first twenty minutes of the day, and all the clients gather in the main media room. It's the whole community together. We start off with a motivational video. It gets the blood flowing, gets their energy up. It gets the clients awake and alert. It's inspiring. We focus on recovery trigger songs that have a tendency to inspire somebody to feel empowered and inspired to want to do something for themselves.

The next session is called the Mic Check group. It's based on one of the principles of the twelve-step program. For example, the principles of humility or acceptance or honesty. There's a whole song list of music on YouTube that we use as resources that correspond to the steps. In addition to recorded music, Recovery Unplugged staff who are professional musicians also perform live music acoustically that is geared towards a specific topic or principle.

Then after that group there is a Caseload group. That's a more intensive process group. That's the group in which I play family dedication songs for clients. That's a very emotional experience. I don't tell them initially who the family dedication is from and who it's for. They are listening to the music, having an open heart and open mind to consider that perhaps this is something that their parents are communicating to them.

After lunch, there are two more groups in the afternoon. There's usually a Recovery Playlist Group where each client provides music that inspires them to look over recovery triggers. Then we have community groups. We also do a lot of improvisational work.

Then they go back to the residence, and they have free time and time to review their written assignments and to get more acquainted with each other. They start developing friendships with the other clients at the residence. Then they go to an open twelve-step meeting every night that they're here. They go to meetings seven days a week. In addition to six hours of programming during the day, clients can do other activities like yoga on the beach, or they can go to the gym and work out.

Are clients surprised by the treatment program at Recovery Unplugged®?
I have a lot of young adults that I work with, and what young adults are so shocked by is the fact that this particular treatment center treats them with the upmost respect. That's not something they have been accustomed to receiving. It's done through the music. When a client first comes in, for example, let's say that he's twenty-four years old and that he has spent the majority of his life in his bedroom listening to his own music and having his parents yell at him, "You need to turn

that music down!" Instead, what I say is, "Before you actually tell me anything about who you are, I want you to play a song for me that will give me a good idea of who you are without you saying anything."

When they play a song for me that gives me a feel for who they are at the core, they get almost giddy about the experience. So, straight out of the gate, we can build rapport with a client immediately by respecting the music that they care about, by respecting something and honoring something about them that only their friends who use have been able to do for them. It lends itself to a really intimate sort of environment. It gets very intimate here very quickly.

You've said that one of the most beautiful things you've seen occur is music bringing Recovery Unplugged® clients and their families together. Can you give an example?
There's a quote on one of the walls at Recovery Unplugged that says, "Where words fail, music speaks." That's exactly what happened in a family session I was leading with a mother, father, and their daughter here in my office. It was going absolutely nowhere. There was so much anguish and so much pain and so much misunderstanding and genuine sadness about their inability to communicate with each other that it started to accelerate to the point of anger.

So I decided to ask the father, who was having probably the most difficult time, to choose a song that he would like to play for his daughter at that moment. From that moment forward, while the music was playing, the defenses broke down immediately. After the song was played, the session changed radically. They were vulnerable with each other. They were able to talk about things that before they had not been able to talk about. It allowed them to actually speak from the heart instead of from the defense mechanisms that they had put together. That was one of the coolest things.

WE ARE FAMILY

Like Sister Sledge, "We are family."

Our connection to our clients continues long after treatment ends. We are proactive about staying in touch with our alumni—or as they would say, about staying in their faces. Our staff is constantly reaching out to graduates, whether they left two weeks ago, two months ago, or any time since our opening back in 2013. Our monthly and quarterly Recovery Unplugged sponsored alumni events serve both to support clients' sobriety and to let us know how they are dealing with the world outside our doors.

The turnout for our annual reunions is incredible. More than one hundred people from all over the country typically show up to celebrate their sobriety. Richie performs, along with past and present clients, and several speakers share their success stories. There are always a lot of tears.

When we see some of those clients—especially the really tough cases—show up, we're absolutely thrilled to see they're still sober. For example, there was one guy who had been to fifteen treatment centers before Recovery Unplugged. By the time he found us, he was a hot mess. There he was at the reunion, sober and smiling.

"Recovery Unplugged was unlike anything I've ever experienced," he said. "People really care. I never realized how powerful music can be in my life."

The reunions are so successful that our alumni are now starting their own chapters and organizing their own musical events all over the country.

RU EVENTS

Alumni gatherings are one way to maintain contact with clients. We also sponsor other recovery activities that are both supportive and entertaining. One of my favorites is "Rappers in Recovery" night, where guest artists perform recovery rap for clean and sober audiences. We have a DJ, and we organize what we call Compliment Battles.

Instead of rapping insults at one another, rappers will be kind and offer support for continued recovery.

In addition, through collaboration with a variety of different organizations and nonprofits, we are involved in sponsoring events all over the country. We've been to California; Michigan; Washington, DC; Ohio; Texas; Massachusetts; Nevada; Louisiana; Arizona; New Jersey; and of course, Florida. We plan to expand these programs in the coming years.

STEVEN TYLER IS A FAN OF WHAT WE DO

Our core philosophy is the cornerstone of our success. The universe has had a hand in creating the buzz and spreading the word.

As luck would have it, our creative director, Richie Supa, just happens to be best friends with rock 'n' roll legend Steven Tyler. Richie asked him to show up at Recovery Unplugged to share his recovery story and perform. Thanks to the Internet and YouTube, more than five million people viewed Steven singing "Amazing" and "Dream On" on our facility stage. It's worth a look; just search YouTube for "Steven Tyler Recovery Unplugged."

Steven's visit to Recovery Unplugged was kept a secret.

Once it was confirmed that he was really coming, Richie swore the entire staff to secrecy. We couldn't even tell our families. Steven wanted to avoid a paparazzi spectacle and keep it real for the clients.

To say we were star-struck would be an understatement. Everyone was so excited that Steven took time out of his busy schedule to visit with our clients and staff.

It was heartwarming to witness the moment when Steven and Richie saw each other for the first time in quite a while; they were hugging each other and tears of happiness were flowing. You could really feel the love. These guys had been through hell together. They had lost so many friends to drugs, and they were just grateful to be alive.

Then everyone went into the group room. Steven sat down in the audience as Richie performed a song.

Then Richie said, "Come on up here, man. Let's play a few songs together."

Steven said jokingly, "What? Are you kidding? We didn't even rehearse."

Richie laughed. "Are you kidding me, man? We've been rehearsing for forty years. Get up here."

Before Steven started singing "Amazing," Richie read a fan letter to the crowd, which consisted of clients and a few staff. Basically, the letter said, "I was getting ready to take a shot of heroin in 1993 and the song 'Amazing' came on the radio. The lyrics kept me from shooting up. I wanted you to know that I just celebrated sixteen years clean."

Now Steven was tearing up because he was so moved by that letter. Richie started playing the first few bars of "Amazing" on the piano, and Steven began to sing. If you watch the video on YouTube, there are times when you can see how emotional Steven is getting. Then he sang "Dream On," hitting those high notes like it was 1973, the year the song came out. The clients were incredibly moved, and they were grateful for Steven's visit, especially for the live performance.

Later, Steven patiently posed for a group photo with our staff, and then after about forty-five minutes, he said, "That's it! No more pictures unless everybody puts a finger in their nose."

We all stood behind him, put our fingers in our noses, and somebody snapped the photo of all of us. We have the picture hanging up in our Florida facility.

As we were leaving the conference room after it was all

over, a new client was standing in the hallway with his bags, waiting to be admitted. He looked up and saw Steven Tyler standing there. The client said, "Uh, I guess I'm in the right place."

Steven hugged him.

Not your typical entry into rehab. Then again, not your typical rehab.

Once we left the facility, Steven said, "I want to be a part of this." He will always be an honorary member of the Recovery Unplugged family. We are grateful for his support of what we're doing.

The reputation we've earned through celebrity endorsements like Steven's has grown because of visits by other artists like Flo Rida, Dion, Morris Day from Morris Day and the Time, Kevin Martin from Candlebox, Aerosmith drummer Joey Kramer, and Ricky Byrd from Joan Jett and the Blackhearts. That celebrity support, combined with our industry-leading results, has launched Recovery Unplugged from relative obscurity to what can only be described as a musical movement.

Now other rehab facilities are attempting to emulate our program on some level. It's a positive development that means the addiction therapy world is heeding our message. People in the industry are finally realizing what we've known all along. As Richie Supa says, "Music is the medicine."

ARE YOU OR A LOVED ONE SUFFERING FROM ADDICTION? CONTACT US.

Call us 24/7 at 1-800-55-REHAB (73422)

or visit our website, RecoveryUnplugged.com.

CLINICIAN Q&A WITH CRYSTAL MAYO, PRIMARY THERAPIST, RECOVERY UNPLUGGED®

MASTER OF SOCIAL WORK

Why did you join Recovery Unplugged®?

One of the reasons was that music has always impacted my life and my ability to not only communicate my feelings but to feel as though I wasn't alone. Anytime I found a song that I felt I could relate to, it was reassuring that I wasn't the only person who was struggling with whatever I was going through in that moment. I figured, "Wow, what a great way for clients to utilize music to explore feelings that they may not otherwise know how to voice."

Why do you say that Recovery Unplugged® helps more than just the clients?

One of the things that I've noticed with the musical component of Recovery Unplugged is that it's a great way to incorporate the clients' family members and loved ones into the recovery process. That's what I think is so interesting about this process, it isn't necessarily just for the clients, but also for the families, who really get into the process as well. It's beautiful to see.

Family structures are a huge trigger for a lot of the clients in regard to their relapse. Some of them are going back to those homes after treatment. Often clients struggle with the idea of even remaining in treatment because of a conflict they had with a family member or a resentment that they were holding onto.

What I found was that the clients' family members were also struggling to communicate their fears, their frustrations, and even their love to the clients. By including family, through family dedications, a lot of the clients let their guard down. The songs can feel really personal. We're often surprised by the message that the family members are sending through songs. It allows for a new door to be opened in terms of their communication or their willingness to try and rebuild family relationships.

The Recovery Unplugged program also helps the staff. When we use the music in our individual and group sessions, it pumps us up, too. It puts us in a better mood, and as a result of that, we're more effective with the clients.

Do the clients need to have musical talent?
Absolutely not. In fact, most of our founders, including Paul Pellinger, have no musical talent or ability to sing. Even the person who came up with the concept of using the power of music to treat addiction has no musical talent, so the clients certainly don't have to either.

But because of our reputation, some clients who come here are nervous because they think, "I hope this isn't a talent show. I don't know how to sing, don't know how to perform." But when they come into treatment and they realize that it's much more of a therapeutic way that we're using the music, that puts them at ease.

Why do you like working at Recovery Unplugged®?
There's a real sense of comfort here. There's a real sense of family here. There's a real emphasis on growth and development here. They really want us to explore other

avenues and trainings, and try to find other ways to reach clients.

Also, Recovery Unplugged staff members are not hired just based on the letters behind their name, their experience, and their résumé. We give equal attention to a candidate's comfort with the treatment concept, and to our gut feelings about them. Because you can't teach passion. You can't teach people to want to help other people. Those things are more important than a résumé. Our selective hiring pays off; satisfaction with our staff is routinely rated above 90 percent in exit interviews with clients.

Do you have a favorite part of the treatment program?

A lot of the groups that we have are very deep and serious. The clients are talking a lot about shame and guilt, negative past behaviors, and resentments. My favorite part is what I call Memories. This is a session where the clients explore positive things that have happened in their lives, and they try to figure out how to continue having those positive experiences. It's nice to balance things out so they can identify a way to have positivity in recovery.

How do you make sure the clients understand the lyrics?

We play the lyric version of each music video, which has the lyrics written on the screen in subtitles. This helps the rest of the group members to connect with the words, rather than just the music. Sometimes I'll play a certain song that everyone has heard on the radio a million times. They say, "I never really knew that those were the lyrics. I never knew that was the meaning behind it." This will spark a discussion about how they relate to the song and what that song means to them.

How does Recovery Unplugged® compare to the other rehab centers you worked at?

I've worked at traditional treatment centers. There is not as much engagement in the traditional rehab facilities as there is at Recovery Unplugged. I remember seeing those clients dread the idea of spending thirty days in treatment. The countdown would begin fairly quickly after a client arrived. I feel like the connections weren't that strong. It's different here. Music is a really powerful thing, the way people can connect to music and how it can build relationships.

How do you know what songs to play and when?

We keep a database called Musical Prescriptions with a list of uplifting songs, motivating songs, or songs based on recovery. We have a folder for each type of topic. If it's about spirituality or relationships or respect, we've got a little bank of songs ready. The entire staff is really good at finding appropriate songs for different situations.

How do you know the Recovery Unplugged® program is working?

We can see it. We can see the results with our own eyes. We have clients who leave here, and they're sober for a year, and they come back and visit because they're so grateful for the support that they receive from Recovery Unplugged. You don't see that much in this industry, you just don't. It's really cool. It's really rewarding. When I see a client after a year and they're like, "Hey, I just wanted to stop by because I wanted to tell you about my life, how good things are going," that's cool.

Tell me more about the support clients get from one another?
The emphasis on the family vibe that we provide here really works. It's something beautiful to see when a client comes in and they're really overwhelmed at first. Then a bunch of the other clients, a bunch of their peers come over, welcome them, and kind of ease them into the process.

I've had a lot of clients who come in, and they're like, "This is my first time in treatment. I wanted to leave as soon as I got here, but then everybody was so welcoming and kind, and I didn't think that was going to happen at treatment. I felt supported right off the bat." That's another thing that separates us from other treatment centers: the fact that the clients feel so comforted so quickly, by people that they don't even know.

CHAPTER FOUR

THE BUSINESS OF TREATMENT AND AVOIDING RELAPSE

The system is broken and people are dying. It's as simple and as horrifying as that. When 97 percent of addicts who have been through some type of rehab are relapsing within a year, it doesn't take a rocket scientist to see that the conventional treatment model is failing. America's 14,500 treatment centers are not even making a dent in a problem that long ago reached epic proportions. The only way to effect real change is to rethink the overall culture of addiction treatment.

A BROKEN SYSTEM

There is so much that is just not right about the business of treatment. Instead of getting clean and moving on to lead productive lives, most clients are statistics, doomed to relapse and continue suffering. We are determined to change the statistics and the industry.

A client of mine from twenty years ago comes to mind. I met him when I was working as a court liaison in the 1990s, long before Recovery Unplugged. He was nineteen years old, maybe 120 pounds, soaking wet. He had never been in treatment before and had gotten arrested for possession of cocaine. I was able to keep him out of jail, but he went into a one-size-fits-all rehab facility where they tried to force him to fit in. He hated it. He left therapy, relapsed, and went on a two-week bender of cocaine and no sleep.

The drugs combined with lack of sleep precipitated a psychotic state. He broke into a banker's house intending to steal money. The robbery turned into a rape and murder and he got the death penalty.

If only the system had known what to do with this kid, that banker might still be alive and that nineteen-year-old kid would not be sitting on death row. It's another case of generic drug rehab that didn't even come close to reaching the client.

AVOIDING RELAPSE

Of course, an addict has to really want to become clean in order for rehab to work. They need to do their part and take responsibility for their own recovery. Eventually, every client has to leave rehab and fend for themselves. That means they need to form healthy habits, find a sponsor, go to meetings, do step work, and commit to bettering themselves. They also need to find out what's really triggering their behavior so they can deal with the underlying emotional cause of their actions.

For some clients, relapse means committing crimes and doing serious jail time. For others, it means death. There have been more deaths from drug overdoses in the last eight years than in the previous eighteen years combined. Before Recovery Unplugged, when that phone would ring in the middle of the night, you could guess what was going to be on the other end of it. It was heartbreaking.

There are a number of reasons for this, one of which is that after staying sober for a period of time, clients will not realize their tolerance level for drugs has dropped. Taking the same amount of a drug they used prior to rehab may be more than their cleaned-out system can metabolize.

There is also a difference in what clients are taking today. Back in the day, somebody would shoot a bag of dope and die from an overdose. Now, they'll take a Percocet with a Xanax—that they can conveniently get from a doctor—chase it down with a shot of whiskey, go to sleep, and never wake up.

When they run out of oxy pills, if they can't renew the prescription, it's cheap and easy to buy heroin. Their friendly neighborhood drug dealers, who used to cut the heroin with harmless baking soda or a powdered laxative, are now mixing the heroin with lethal poisons like fentanyl, which makes the mixture about a hundred times stronger than morphine. Whether users ingest it, shoot it, or snort it, it's killing them. There's an epidemic going on. It's dramatic and it's making national news. See Chapter 6 for more information on the high costs of the addiction epidemic.

CHANGING THE CONVERSATION

What's astounding is that with all the focus and hand-wringing about relapsing, overdosing, and death, there is no conversation about assessing the ineptitude of conventional therapy and finding a more effective solution. This may harken back to addiction still being treated as the bastard child of the mental health profession. People need to realize that only three percent of addicts fit the stereotypical skid-row profile. To describe the rest, all you have to do is look at your friends and neighbors. Ninety-seven percent of drug addicts look like everybody else.

When you realize that the people who have stigmatized drug addiction as a poor choice instead of as a disease are the same ones setting the model to treat addiction, you can see the conflict of interest. Doctors may go to medical school for seven years, but in that time, they get only eight hours of education on addiction, which is officially still called "chemical dependency." Addiction isn't dependency—it's a disease.

Medical professionals, psychologists, and psychiatrists are trained to focus on addiction etiologies, the causal factors. Understanding that growing up with a father who constantly called you a piece of shit destroyed your self-esteem and started the addiction cycle is not necessarily going to change your behavior today. The real question is, how are you going to deal with the reality of the present? Again, the mantra of Recovery Unplugged is how do we make recovery a bigger payoff than getting high?

THE TRUTH ABOUT RELAPSE

Once a client uses again after a period of being clean, we call that relapse. The truth is, relapse starts even before the person actually picks up the drug. It can be caused by any of the universal relapse triggers. Certain people and places—different for everybody—are on that list. Money—having too much or too little—can also be a trigger.

Boredom can be the problem. What is boredom but too much focus on yourself? When people do nothing but focus on themselves, they can easily relapse. Nobody will argue that it is important for clients to steer clear of those relapse triggers, but what is equally important is to focus on the recovery triggers.

If an addict's only tools when they leave rehab are avoidance of their relapse triggers and the fear of consequences if they start using again, they will be anxious and miserable, waiting for the other shoe to drop. Why stay clean if they're going to be miserable? There will inevitably come a point when the addict will be so depressed that it will be easy for them to say, "You know what? I am so depressed, so fearful, so anxious, and having such a tough time living life on life's terms that I might as well just go use. But this time, I'll only drink. I won't shoot heroin."

Or once the addict's drugs and alcohol are gone, and all that's left is the angst, they will start doctor shopping in search of a prescription for Xanax. They may feel better in the short term, but now they're taking pills again. As the Demi Lovato song "Here We Go Again" describes, the downward spiral begins. Whatever progress was made in rehab is completely undone.

AVOIDING RELAPSE

The key to successfully avoiding relapse is to find recovery triggers that reinforce contentment, gratitude, optimism, and self-confidence. Instead of taking that defensive posture and expending so much energy avoiding negatives, why not go on the offense looking for positive feelings? Instead of sitting in fear of consequences, the idea is to be proactive in creating a restorative atmosphere conducive to healing and staying clean. Though we support the twelve-step approach that teaches humility and respect for a disease that can get you anytime, feeling good about yourself and developing a more positive image of yourself is imperative in recovery.

There is no more positive recovery trigger than music. It is the only form of communication that consistently touches the soul. We can talk clients into a coma, but words don't reach our inner depths the way music does.

Heal the soul and affect a long-lasting change from the inside out. That is the key to Recovery Unplugged. We are taking advantage of all aspects of music to involve all the senses. We're reaching clients through musical vibration, specific and meaningful lyrics, live performances, and original compositions.

Music helps clients get in touch with difficult emotions. It can be used as a go-to when they need to find gratitude or be reminded of the horror show life was when they were using. It is the helping hand that keeps clients anchored to the present, stabilizes their mood, and reminds them that recovery is the preferred life.

Recovery Unplugged is finally presenting a viable alternative to the system that is failing so miserably. We are part of the solution. Clients are getting it and staying clean.

ARE YOU OR A LOVED ONE SUFFERING FROM ADDICTION? CONTACT US.

Call us 24/7 at 1-800-55-REHAB (73422)

or visit our website, RecoveryUnplugged.com.

CLINICIAN Q&A WITH NAKITA CHARLES, CLINICAL SUPERVISOR, RECOVERY UNPLUGGED®

BACHELOR OF SCIENCE IN PSYCHOLOGY,
MASTER OF SCIENCE IN FAMILY THERAPY

Has working at Recovery Unplugged® been an inspiration to you?

Absolutely. With all the bad news we see in today's society, I think we tend to forget that there is also much good in humanity. We're working with a population of people who are labeled as junkies, who are labeled as good-for-nothing alcoholics, crack-heads, and all these other negative names, and most of the world tends to lose hope in them. When they're here and we're working with them and we see their transformations, it gives you hope in humanity. It makes you feel like, "If I am able to help this person, then maybe I am doing something to change the world for the better."

Can the clients share their own playlists in group sessions?

Yes. We have wireless networks in all of our group rooms. The clients can play a song from their smartphone onto the sound system in the group rooms. Sometimes we'll also pull up the lyrics. We all have remote controls so that we can access pretty much any song that's related to any topic. We also have a YouTube channel where we have different topics, for example, depression, anxiety, willingness, or love. Within each of these topics we have different videos that are related to it.

Does everyone like music?

You know, that was one of my concerns when coming to work here. "Is everybody going to like the music?" Even the ones that say they don't like music, the music always reaches them. There's always that one song. There are always those songs that are powerful within their lives or that have touched them in some way. I think the music connects to anyone and everyone. That's what's so magical and so powerful about it.

How central is music to the Recovery Unplugged
treatment program?
Music is the heartbeat and the life of Recovery Unplugged. It's not an add-on or an extracurricular. I think that's really what helps us continue to grow. That's what makes the clients want to come back. There are days when the clients just don't want to talk. Maybe they've had a really crappy day. Then we'll start playing songs. It will take them aback and totally catch them off guard. We end up talking for longer than we probably would have, just based off of a song that they liked when they were little.

How do you find out what songs the clients like?
We have a form they fill out titled "Songs of Life." They fill that out, and they write in all the different songs related to different topics in their life. The really cool thing is that by the end of their treatment, they're asking for their peers' songs. Not only have they created a positive memory while they've been here, by the end of it they're asking for the original songs created by their peers. They want to keep those moments with them. It goes to show how much this process is working. For them to want to take those songs with them, and forever remember that experience, that breakthrough,

that maybe one of their peers provided them, that's really awesome to me.

Why are Feel Good Fridays so important?

Feel Good Friday is like a huge party. You never know if a Grammy-winning recording artist or rock star might show up and perform.

Feel Good Fridays are all about feeling good and enjoying life. One of the things about Recovery Unplugged is that we don't focus on the relapse triggers. We focus on recovery triggers. Feel Good Fridays are all about feeling happy. We'll have guest musicians come in. It's all about enjoying and embracing your life and really being grateful for the things that you have. Because, to be quite frank, nobody's getting sober or clean to be miserable.

My office is not too far from the main group room, and I can hear Feel Good Fridays vibrating through the walls. The clients get up, they're dancing—they've even developed several dances to the songs. Sometimes I'll be on a call with families, and they'll be singing along on the phone, so it's really about just enjoying life. I mean, literally the name describes it all: Feel Good Fridays. It's not just a feel good Friday; it's a feel good every day, but Fridays we kick it up ten notches.

Does it help for a client to have musical talent at Recovery Unplugged®?

I would say Recovery Unplugged works just as well, sometimes even better, for the person who isn't a musician. That's a common misconception that a lot of clients and families have. I've been asked, "Does my kid need to be a musician?" I say absolutely not. I've actually connected clients who aren't musicians with clients who are, and they've composed beautiful songs together.

We also do a lot of spoken word or freeform writing. So no, they don't have to be a musician. I've actually had clients that knew nothing about any musical instrument, and by the end of their treatment, they know how to play the guitar, or they know how to play the piano. I had a client that came in thirty minutes to an hour each day before groups, and he sat there and he played the piano. He just started putting different sounds together, and he composed his own song. That's phenomenal to me. That's a coping skill right there.

We also have many clients who do have musical talent, and some are professional musicians. We help those clients harness their talent as a catalyst for long-term recovery by changing their message. Instead of singing about drugs or life in the streets or misogynistic and chauvinistic themes, we encourage them to write lyrics about how they persevered, overcame addiction, and came out better on the other side.

Where do you think recovery and treatment will be ten years from now?
I hope ten years from now that anybody and every-body who needs treatment for substance abuse will be able to get it. I hope there's no one that's turned away because they can't afford it. I hope that people stop using the traditional methods of treatment. I hope people will be more open to that in ten years and more open to places like Recovery Unplugged that are using

other ways. Instead of focusing on the problem, I hope people start focusing on the lives that these clients can live. A lot of times, they lose hope. We're providing them hope. We're helping them find hope in themselves.

CHAPTER FIVE

HOW MUSIC AND DRUGS AFFECT THE BRAIN

Addiction is a brain disease. Addicts are basically assaulting their bodies and brains with chemical warfare. Over time, continued substance abuse can actually change the way the brain is wired.

There is a process called adaptation, in which the brain tries to function normally by compensating for and adapting to the unnatural presence of a harmful chemical substance. In the beginning, the use of drugs may be a deliberate choice. After extended substance abuse, neurological changes occur in the brain that may decrease the individual's ability to make a conscious choice of whether to use or not use.

When an addict stops using, they're left with neurological, physiological, and emotional chaos. As their bodies and brains try to achieve balance, called homeostasis, the medical profession jumps in with antidepressants, sleeping aids, and antianxiety drugs. These are just temporary Band-Aids that do not solve the long-term issues. Plus, they can cause a host of other problems. There is no real change taking place when you just swap one drug for another, even though one may be legal and the other illegal.

In contrast, music can be the catalyst for the real change that restores balance and keeps clients centered and in the present.

MUSIC AND MANKIND

Every human culture in history, and even long before recorded history, has created and played music. Some of the earliest relics of prehistoric man are musical instruments made from animal bone. Often music was played for ceremonial purposes, for communication over distances, or for pure entertainment.

In our modern technological society, it's never been easier to find, download, play, and enjoy exactly the music you want to listen to. The result is that music is more a part of our lives than ever before in human history. According to Edison Research's "Share of Ear" study, most Americans listen to about four hours of music every day.

We listen to music to relax, to exercise, to celebrate, to get romantic, to study, to drive, to get married, to mourn, and a million other reasons. Music is the sound wave of our soul. It's connective energy that triggers our emotions. It calms us. It opens another part of ourselves. It can fix what's broken.

Music is the soundtrack of our lives. Everybody on the planet has a favorite song. Music can have an immediate effect on the human mind and body. Play a song with a catchy tune, and even a young toddler who can barely walk will start to sway and dance to the beat. It's no surprise, then, that the way music affects us is hardwired deep inside the human brain.

NEURAL PATHWAYS

Since music is so universal and so prevalent in our lives, scientists have long theorized that there must be a certain area of the brain specifically designed to receive and interpret music, but they could never find it. In 2016 researchers at the Massachusetts Institute of Technology made a breakthrough. Using hi-tech brain imaging technology, they found brain cells that form neural pathways that react only to the sound of music.

Remarkably, their findings indicate that these musical pathways in the human brain react to virtually any kind of music, regardless of style. Yet they are not triggered by other continuous noises like human speech, lawnmower noise, traffic noise, or waves crashing on a beach.

A music researcher at Georgetown University, Dr. Josef Rauschecker, said, "Music works as a group cohesive. Music-making with other people in your tribe is a very ancient, human thing to do." Perhaps these technical studies of music and the brain partly explain why Recovery Unplugged has tapped into such a powerful treatment for addiction. If the music pathways of the human brain are millions of years old, and addiction is only a few thousand years old, maybe music has the advantage.

THE EFFECT OF MUSIC ON THE BRAIN

Even though individuals may prefer different styles of music and different artists, a study published in the *European Journal of Neuroscience* found similar brain activity patterns in people listening to the same piece of music. A news article on CNN.com quoted the lead author of the study, Daniel Abrams from Stanford University, who said,

"Despite our idiosyncrasies in listening, the brain experiences music in a very consistent fashion across subjects."

That same CNN article summarized the *European Journal of Neuroscience* study, writing, "This suggests that the participants not only perceive the music the same way, but, despite whatever personal differences they brought to the table, there's a level on which they share a common experience." Perhaps this begins to explain the powerful communal results we witness in the Recovery Unplugged group sessions.

Many studies about the effect of music on the human brain indicate that music can be as powerful or even more powerful than traditional pharmaceuticals, such as antianxiety medications. One such study involved hospital patients who were about to undergo surgery, something known to cause high stress, worry, and anxiety. Half of the study participants took antianxiety medications, while the other half simply listened to music.

Researchers found that the patients who listened to music reported lower levels of anxiety. This group also had lower levels of cortisol, a stress hormone. Daniel J. Levitin, author of the bestselling book *This Is Your Brain on Music*, summarized the findings this way: "Music is arguably less expensive than drugs, and it's easier on the body and it doesn't have side effects."

Levitin's research also indicates that listening to music can increase immunoglobulin A in the bloodstream. Immunoglobulin A is an antibody believe to strengthen the immune system. His research also links music to boosting the number of germ- and bacteria-fighting cells in the human body.

THE HEALING POWER OF MUSIC

We really don't need scientific studies to prove the healing power of music. The concept of music as a healing influence that could positively impact health and behavior is as old as the writings of Aristotle and Plato. Yet, to date, nobody is taking advantage of music's power to transform the soul the way we are. Music has always been just an add-on to traditional therapy, never the therapeutic tour de force that it is at Recovery Unplugged. For us, music is the treatment.

Similarly to getting high, music enhances the pleasure centers of the brain, increasing dopamine levels and releasing endorphins. If you monitor brain activity after exposure to crack cocaine, certain key areas of the brain will light up. Those same areas will be activated when the brain hears a musical chord change or a specific inspirational song.

When an addict is using, no matter how hard it is to score drugs and keep the lifestyle going, that shot of heroin provides an immediate euphoric payoff. It takes just as much, if not more, effort to stay clean, so we need to provide an equally appealing payoff. The way in which music impacts our brain's pleasure center creates a natural high, making music the perfect substitute for the drug.

Music connects with the brain's hardwired reward system. Our response to it is natural and visceral—involuntary, not conscious. That is the pure gold of Recovery Unplugged.

In traditional therapy, in order to be open-minded to the therapist's input, you have to choose to surrender. If you don't, therapy will fail. Our relationship with music is so natural that it will transcend whatever intellectual barriers clients throw up. They may come in broken, depressed, angry, and looking for a fight, with their heads resistant to rehab, but their hearts can't resist the musical medicine.

Time after time, we see even the most reluctant clients connecting with lyrics that remind them of who they were on drugs and who they can aspire to be sober. They learn to use music to soothe their souls and stay focused on recovery. It gradually becomes the front line of defense against relapse. The process is truly magical.

GOOD VIBRATIONS

It's not just the music that triggers a response. The term "kicking heroin" is a reference to the jumpy legs that cause you to kick when you're in withdrawal. We've witnessed it countless times, and some of the Recovery Unplugged staff have experienced it firsthand.

When we play some old-school hip-hop with heavy bass in it, the vibration from the bass literally penetrates through the legs, providing temporary relief from the jumpiness. Along with the lyrics, the live performances, the associations, the anchors, and the message, the vibration is having its own impact. Just like in the Gloria Estefan song, the "Rhythm Is Gonna Get You!"

MUSIC AND RECOVERY

It's a fact that music releases dopamine in your brain. It changes your heart rate. It gives you a physical rush of pleasure. It changes your mood and can reduce anxiety. That's why music has been used for years in hospitals for pain management. Music has been used to treat Alzheimer's disease and dementia. But it was never tested for recovery.

In the context of therapy, music can teach clients how to stay away from drugs by showing them where they've been, what they did to themselves, and how they don't have to go back there. A song may trigger the memory of that dirty apartment or that bedroom that they were holed up in with the blinds pulled down. The music can make that recollection so vivid that clients can almost taste it and smell it. That's the power of music that's created and written correctly.

Music is the drug. It's addictive. It's medicine. They say music cleanses the soul of the dirt of everyday life. We believe that's true.

When an addict first comes to treatment, he or she is angry, broken, and shut down. They sit down with their arms crossed over their chest, which is a sign of closing out any outside energy. The last thing they need is somebody shaking a finger at them, saying, "Let me tell you what happens to your brain on drugs." They don't want to hear it.

What we have found at Recovery Unplugged is that music, because it is so nonthreatening, is the perfect catalyst for change. It allows clients to come in and immediately feel comfortable. They let their guard down. They feel connected. They know the words to songs and they sing the choruses together.

Picture a whole group of clients singing, "You Can't Call

This Livin' when You're Busy Dyin'," which is from a song written by our own Richie Supa. They cry when they hear that song because it encapsulates their experience. That song has brought them face-to-face with the effects of their drug use.

When they are using, addicts have no conscience. They don't care about themselves or anybody else. They're not good at living. They're good at dying. They know how to kill themselves, but they don't care because they don't have a conscience.

In the treatment center, when clients are clean, we play these songs, and it reminds them of what they've done. When they're high, they can't see their disease because they're immersed in it. They are blind to it. The only way to see the disease is to stop using. It is only when they put the drugs down and get into recovery that they begin to have a conscience again.

Music separates the disease from the soul. Once you can spot your disease through a song, you can reach out and choke it. That's what we do. Recovery Unplugged is changing the face of how we recover.

ARE YOU OR A LOVED ONE SUFFERING FROM ADDICTION? CONTACT US.

Call us 24/7 at 1-800-55-REHAB (73422)

or visit our website, RecoveryUnplugged.com.

THE ADDICTION EPIDEMIC

As you just read in the preceding chapters, there is a better way to treat addiction. You or your loved one can succeed and get clean. Whether you're an addict yourself or you're reading this book because someone you love is struggling with addiction, there is good news. You can beat this awful disease. You can win. You can get your life and your family back. That's the good news.

But now...the bad news.

Addiction in America is the worst it's ever been. Harmful new drugs that are synthesized in offshore labs are flooding into this country and causing catastrophic destruction and death. According to a Columbia University study, more than 40 million Americans age twelve and over meet the clinical criteria for addiction. Forty million. That's more than one out of every ten people in the US. Another 80 million Americans are categorized as "risky substance abusers" that use alcohol and drugs in ways that threaten health and safety.

THE HIGH COST OF ADDICTION

The financial costs of the addiction epidemic are stunning. By some estimates, the cost of addiction to federal, state, and local governments exceeds $450 billion each year. That cost is paid by taxpayers. It does *not* include the financial costs to families, individuals, employers, and private insurance companies for treatment, counseling, rehabilitation, court costs and legal fees, lost time at work, medical care, emergency room visits, and so on.

But of course it is the human costs where addiction is most profoundly felt. Drugs are the number one cause of accidental death in the United States, and the number of drug-related deaths is increasing every year. A National Institute on Drug Abuse study found that overdose deaths in the US increased by 200 percent between 2000 and 2015. In 2000, 17,415 people died from drug overdoses; in 2015 overdose deaths totaled 52,404.

That's more than the number of people who die in car

crashes, murders, or suicides. The fastest growing category is overdose deaths from opioids, which include heroin and narcotics like oxycodone, fentanyl, morphine, and methadone. According to the Centers for Disease Control, opioid-related deaths increased a whopping 439 percent between 1999 and 2014. CDC's data points out that opioids caused more than 33,000 deaths in 2015 alone, the most recent year for which statistics are available.

A report by CNN stated that "the sharp uptick in deaths seems to coincide with Americans' increasing use of drugs like illicit fentanyl." Fentanyl is a powerful synthetic opioid that is up to one hundred times more potent than morphine and fifty times more powerful than heroin. Recording artist Prince died of a fentanyl overdose in 2016.

Death from overdose is just one of the many human and social costs of addiction. Many thousands of drug users contract needle-borne illnesses such as HIV/AIDS and hepatitis. The CDC estimates that more than 120,000 people currently living with AIDS in the United States contracted the disease from injecting drugs.

Addiction can also lead to violent crimes, property crimes, domestic abuse, child abuse, unplanned pregnancy, motor-vehicle accidents, jail and prison time, as well as financial and legal problems. An unknown number of families and individuals face financial ruin and bankruptcy due to addiction.

Drug addiction can destabilize and destroy families. Children of addicts are often abused or neglected as a result of the parents' need for drugs. Children whose parents or other family members abuse drugs often fail to receive proper medical care, dental care, nutrition, immunizations, and education, and are sometimes physically or emotionally abused. Between 50 and 80 percent of child abuse and neglect cases involve drug abuse by parents, according to the National Institute on Drug Abuse.

Drug addicts also can put at risk people other than direct family members. Many addicts cannot get or hold a job, but those who do work put others at risk. In 2016, drug-testing company Quest Diagnostics reported that the number of American workers testing positive for drugs has been increasing steadily over the past three years and is at a ten-year high. Quest Diagnostics also found that nearly 6 percent of workers who were involved in on-the-job employment-related accidents tested positive for drugs.

Employees who abuse drugs sometimes steal money or property from their employer in order to sell them for cash to buy drugs. Other negative effects on employers include decreased productivity, increased absenteeism, and extensive use of the employer's medical insurance, which drives up costs.

Of course, the person who suffers most is the drug addict himself. Addiction can lead to a wide range of health problems, including anxiety and depression, mental illness, brain damage, physical illness, internal organ failure, malnutrition, high blood pressure, heart disease and stroke, accidents and injuries, risk of infectious diseases due to needle-sharing, sexual side effects, STDs, and so on.

Addiction also affects the addict's social relationships with others, and increases the chances of being put in a dangerous situation that causes undue risks to oneself or to others. Addicts often face financial problems and debts. In order to pay off debts, the addict might be forced into illegal activities such as theft, robbery, violence, or prostitution. Drug addiction can lead to spending so much money on drugs that there is nothing left over to pay basic living expenses like food and rent, which can lead to homelessness.

FEAR OF OVERDOSING

One of the most terrifying trends in drug addiction today is the addition of Carfentanyl laced into heroin. Carfentanyl is a synthetic opioid used to sedate elephants, and it's so powerful that just a few specs the size of a grain of sugar can be deadly. It's ten thousand times more potent than morphine. Drug cartels began lacing heroin with Carfentanyl because it's cheap and easy to produce in a lab, and when cut into heroin, it makes the heroin more potent and more addictive.

Drug enforcement agencies suspect Carfentanyl is being manufactured in China, then ordered online via the Dark Web and shipped to Mexican cartels or other gangs, who mix it with heroin and then smuggle it into the United States. When Carfentanyl started showing up laced into heroin, overdose deaths skyrocketed. In one county in Ohio, there were forty-eight heroin overdoses in a single day due to Carfentanyl.

Significantly, the fear of overdosing has become a key factor to why many more addicts are now seeking treatment. Every week in the news, we read about more and more overdose deaths caused by heroin laced with lethal fillers and contaminants. Addicts are beginning to realize that any time they stick a needle in their arm, it could be their last.

Law enforcement officials across the country say this is the worst drug-addiction epidemic they have ever seen. The illegal drugs coming across the border are more addictive and deadly than ever before. One criminal prosecutor in Ohio summarized the solution this way: "We can't just say it's a crime and lock people up. You have to engage hospitals and addiction treatment centers and try to get people out of this cycle."

At Recovery Unplugged we couldn't agree more. Which is why we broke the mold of the traditional treatment center and forged our own unique solution to addiction and recovery. In the next chapter, we'll take a brief look into the history of how addiction has been treated for decades, and why conventional therapies are not working.

ARE YOU OR A LOVED ONE SUFFERING FROM ADDICTION? CONTACT US.

Call us 24/7 at 1-800-55-REHAB (73422)

or visit our website, RecoveryUnplugged.com.

THE HISTORY OF REHAB AND RECOVERY UNPLUGGED®

Recovery Unplugged is special. Our philosophy is unique. Our results are exceptional and far exceed industry norms. We'll continue to get even better in the future. In order to fully understand how Recovery Unplugged differs from other treatment and rehab facilities, it will be helpful to review the past. This chapter contains a brief history of drug and alcohol rehabilitation in America, and it ends with a discussion of why conventional rehab treatments no longer work.

ADDICTION HAS PLAGUED MANKIND FOR MILLENNIA

Addiction is not a new phenomenon. Human history is full of examples of cultures and societies that abused substances in order to feel good or get high. In fact, addiction has plagued humankind for thousands of years. Wine was used as a drug by the ancient Egyptians. Narcotics were prevalent as early as 4,000 BC. Marijuana was cultivated as a medicinal herb in China almost 5,000 years ago. The phenomenon of humans becoming addicted to chemical substances is not new. What has changed is the way we have reacted to and treated addiction throughout history.

Alcohol has been used in various ways by humans since before recorded history. Before the arrival of European settlers in North America, Native Americans used fermented alcohol, but only as part of ritual ceremonies. They did not drink alcohol as a recreational beverage or to get drunk. So they had no need for any form of rehab to help tribe members overcome alcoholism. That changed later when white settlers began trading with Native Americans, offering wine and distilled spirits in exchange for land, furs, and other valuable resources.

Those early European settlers were, by and large, religious communities, many fleeing religious persecution and seeking a new life in the New World. Addiction was common among these settlers, primarily to alcohol and spirits. Addiction was seen as a moral failing, and the most common treatment for alcohol addiction was found in religion. Early addiction therapy was based on using religious beliefs and morality as a way to encourage people to avoid the evil state of drunkenness.

One type of addiction therapy used by both Native Americans and settlers was called a sobriety circle. Community elders and alcoholics would form a circle in an attempt to show a united front and scare off the evil spirits that were believed to be the cause of alcoholism. Those who were addicted to alcohol were taught to appeal to God, read the Bible, and seek the spiritual realm to ask for the strength to avoid drinking. As you can imagine, these early treatment strategies resulted in mixed success.

MORPHINE AND OTHER DRUGS

In addition to alcohol, other drugs were common in early American history, including forms of cocaine, morphine, opium, and heroin. Doctors and field medics during the Civil War used morphine as a painkiller for soldiers wounded on the battlefield. The intense pain of bullet and cannon wounds required large doses of morphine for weeks. As a result, many historians believe that up to 45,000 injured Civil War soldiers became addicted to morphine and needed regular doses in order to function.

Also in the late 1800s, many women became addicted to opioid drugs. These drugs were not well understood at the time, and they were used in common medications for women, such as medicine to reduce menstrual pain and morning sickness. When a patient became addicted to a certain medication, most doctors would try to treat the problem by simply switching the patient to a different medication. But opiates were widespread, and often doctors would simply swap one addictive medicine for another, with little benefit to the patient.

During this time, most narcotics were newly discovered, misunderstood, and totally unregulated. Physicians prescribed them freely for many different health maladies. You could even buy narcotics through the mail or at the corner drug store.

To make matters worse, a total lack of understanding of addiction led to much suffering and hardship for those who became addicted. Religious beliefs still dominated the thinking about addiction. Many community leaders and clergy believed that addiction was a choice, and that people who became addicts simply lacked a strong faith in God or sufficient morals. When prayer and religious cures failed to work, punishment for addicts was harsh. Many addicts ended up in prison or, worse, in sanitariums or mental hospitals.

A CHANGE IN BELIEFS

The disastrous consequences of addiction gradually became apparent and slowly gained public awareness. It took until 1875 for the first laws to be passed. That was the year opium dens were outlawed in San Francisco.

Common belief during this time held that addicts could stop their destructive behavior by willfully making a choice to stop. That all changed when Benjamin Rush, now known as the father of psychiatry, observed the flaws in this belief and stated his findings. He theorized that the chemical makeup of alcohol and its physiological effect on the human body led to addiction. Rush put forth the notion that addiction is a disease, and he called for hospitals to create "sober houses" to treat addicts. He believed that the only cure for addiction was to wean oneself off of the addictive substance, and ultimately to stop drinking alcohol or using all together.

Soon, sober houses, also sometimes called inebriate asylums, became common in America. Their goal was to treat people addicted to alcohol and drugs. Those treatments were not necessarily successful, and they were often brutal. One common treatment strategy of the day was to punish alcoholics and addicts so they would no longer drink or use. This often involved mental and physical abuse, including aversion therapy, hydrotherapy, and electric therapy.

In addition to alcoholism, drug addiction also became common during this time period. By the turn of the century, an estimated two hundred thousand people were addicted to cocaine. In the late 1800s sober houses and inebriate asylums also began treating drug addicts. The state of New York was one of the first to open a network of rehab facilities to treat both alcohol and drug addiction. In addition to cocaine, addicts also abused chloroform, ether, opium, and morphine.

Private treatment facilities soon opened. The most well-known were called Keeley Institutes. Founder Leslie Keeley believed that addiction was a disease and the cure was pharmacological. Although the Keeley therapies were kept secret, Keeley Institutes would reportedly inject patients with a mixture of bichloride of gold, morphine, arsenic, strychnine, ammonia, atropine, and other toxic ingredients. The side effects were brutal, and included relapse, insanity, and even death. Some researchers believe that in extreme cases, the Keeley Institutes would also perform lobotomies and bloodletting in an attempt to cure addicts.

Despite the harsh therapies and low success rate, historians credit Keeley with developing several good ideas for the treatment of addiction. First was the idea of the thirty-day stay in an inpatient treatment facility so addicts could concentrate solely on recovery. Second was a focus on health and nutrition during an inpatient stay. According to witnesses, patients who went into Keeley Institutes received daily exercise and healthy, nutritious meals. Third, Keeley also pioneered the concept of having recovered addicts work with the patients as a source of motivation and counseling. Poor success rates and lasting side effects of the toxic injections led to the closure of all Keeley Institutes by 1925.

COCAINE AS TREATMENT

Many doctors and psychiatrists throughout history recommended treating addictions with other drugs. For example, Sigmund Freud, among others, believed that cocaine should be used as a cure for alcoholism and morphine addiction. Drug stores in Freud's day would carry home-remedy kits to treat excessive drinking and drug addiction. These kits often contained other damaging and addictive drugs in addition to cocaine, such as opium and marijuana.

In the early 1900s, the US Congress passed laws to regulate the harmful remedies for treating addiction. In 1905, Congress banned opium. Shortly after that, in 1906, Congress created the Pure Food and Drug Act, requiring pharmaceutical companies to affix labels to medications that listed the ingredients.

Eight years later, in 1914, the Harrison Narcotic Act restricted the sale of medicines containing cocaine or opiates only to licensed pharmacies and doctors. In 1923, the US government banned all previously legal narcotics, including cocaine and heroin. Eventually, the US Supreme Court made it illegal for doctors to knowingly prescribe narcotics to addicts, and some doctors were even jailed. By the 1920s, this made addictive drugs more difficult to get but also led to the rise of the illegal drug trade and black market.

ALCOHOLICS ANONYMOUS

Dr. Bob Smith and Bill Wilson founded Alcoholics Anonymous in 1935. Their famous Twelve-Step program has helped millions of alcoholics find sobriety. Three main elements of AA are that alcoholics benefit from the support of others struggling with the same addiction, that alcoholics must take recovery one day at a time, and that overcoming addiction requires faith in a higher power.

The first AA meetings happened in 1939 in New York, and soon the Twelve-Step program spread all over the world. The success of Alcoholics Anonymous also spawned other addiction groups, including Narcotics Anonymous, Gamblers Anonymous, and even Overeaters Anonymous. The Twelve-Step program is spiritually based, but secular and agnostic groups also exist to help those who are uncomfortable with the spiritual elements of AA.

One of the first women to complete the Alcoholics Anonymous Twelve-Step program was named Marty Mann. She dedicated her life to changing the public and government perceptions of alcoholism. Specifically, she fought against the notion that addiction was a moral failing and not a medical condition. She helped create the National Committee for Education on Alcoholism, which strived to show that alcoholism was a disease, that alcoholics were sick, that they deserved medical treatment, and that they could be cured.

THERAPEUTIC COMMUNITIES, BETTY FORD, AND THE EXPANSION OF TREATMENT CENTERS

The 1960s saw the advent of something called therapeutic communities. They were created as an alternative to prison. At that time, the prison system was filling up with addicts, so they created therapeutic communities for nonviolent offenders. They were more like military boot camps. The original therapeutic community was called Synanon. The majority of clients were heroin addicts. These were not short-term thirty-day programs like the rehab centers of today; they were typically one- or two-year programs. I actually went to a therapeutic community in the 1980s, and I'll tell you a little more about my experience a little later in this chapter.

Once addiction was accepted as a disease, treatment began to take root in the medical community, and addicts could now receive therapy in hospitals and clinics. US President Richard Nixon began federal government funding for drug treatment programs. The next US president, Gerald Ford, had personal experience with addiction when his wife, Betty Ford, struggled with substance abuse. In 1982, she established the world-famous Betty Ford Clinic to help those struggling with alcoholism and addiction to prescription medications. After the success and publicity surrounding the Betty Ford Clinic, drug and alcohol rehabilitation centers began to open across the country.

Today there are approximately 14,500 drug and alcohol treatment facilities in the United States. Too many of them have their priorities mixed up; they're in the business of making money first, saving lives second. At Recovery Unplugged our mission is to save lives. Period.

The number 14,500 may seem large, but with 22 million Americans who need treatment, it's not enough. In 2014, only about 2.5 million people received treatment—just over 10 percent of those who need it.

Addiction continues to be a growing problem in America, and a difficult one to solve. The good news is that treatment for addiction has come a long way from the days of sobriety circles. Mounting medical evidence and improved data are showing us what is working and what isn't. Unfortunately, many of the conventional therapies used in rehab centers today are not working.

Successful treatment requires a multifaceted approach, which typically includes education, detox, individual therapy, group therapy, family counseling, behavioral modification, psychiatry, medication, nutrition, and exercise. In addition to these common elements, we strongly believe in adding music therapy into the mix.

Addiction treatment often requires an inpatient stay in a facility for a period of twenty-eight days or more. It always requires a strategy to help the patient stay clean and sober once they return to their everyday life. This involves helping the patient learn to cope with stress, family, job, friends, and the triggers that could lead to relapse. This is one of the most common places where traditional therapy fails. We believe music is an effective tool to accomplish this.

THE ORIGINS OF RECOVERY UNPLUGGED®

I had been thinking about the concept of using music in addiction therapy for more than twenty years. Before opening Recovery Unplugged, I had been part of the rehab community for over two decades, as both a clinician and a client. I also facilitated the opening of dozens of treatment centers in South Florida. I've seen in my own life the healing power of music.

I am not a musician, nor do I have any musical talent. I just know that in my fifty-plus years of life, music has always been—and will always be—my friend. A song will make me remember my parents' twenty-fifth wedding anniversary or spark memories of my first girlfriend. Music is the key to the safe deposit box of my life's memories. I know I am not unique in that regard. Music has a universal impact, which is what makes Recovery Unplugged so effective. The beauty of music as a therapeutic tool is its ability to connect to any client, of any age, at any stage of life.

I grew up ten miles from the original Woodstock site in the Catskill Mountains, a rural area in upstate New York. I didn't realize it back then, but it's known as an energy vortex and spiritual hub that attracts, among others, Hasidic Jews, Zen Buddhists, and back in the day, of course, Woodstock-bound hippies. There was a whole vibe going on up there that I didn't really understand. I'm sure if you talk to somebody tuned into the metaphysical, they'd say the vibration of that whole area influenced who I am today. I feel I was almost destined to spread that healing energy and help people break the cycle of addiction.

MUSICAL MEMORIES

Music was always part of the picture. I can't remember what happened forty-five minutes ago, but I vividly recall dancing around my parents' restaurant forty-five years ago like it was yesterday. At five years old, every time somebody would play a song on the jukebox, I would instinctively start to dance. The customers really dug it. They would come in, my parents would put me on the table, and I would feel the music and just dance. I'm sure there were many songs I loved, but my particular favorite was "Yummy, Yummy, Yummy," performed by Ohio Express in 1968. I can clearly remember being on the table and watching the response from my family and the customers. They felt good, and I felt good making them feel good. That was the beginning of my processing just how powerful music could be in making people happy.

When he was young, my dad was a dance teacher. He turned me on to a wide variety of songs by all sorts of artists, including Bill Haley and the Comets, the Carpenters, Tony Orlando and Dawn, Barry Manilow, and Dion. But when my family and I were dancing around the house, it was always to the Jackson 5.

Early on, I associated music with good times, with innocence, with happiness, with watching my father dance with my mother. He'd swing her to the left side, then to the right side, then between his legs. It was so cool. I remember thinking, "Wow, this is fun."

The power of music still amazes me, even in adulthood. For example, one day at a stoplight several years ago, I saw an elderly gentleman sitting in the car next to me. He looked a little down, so I decided to try something. I put on some Ray Charles, turned up the volume, and boom.

He looked at me and said, "They don't make it like that anymore." Right away I could see his mood changing. I didn't have to say a word to him.

MUSICAL TRIGGERS

While music has certainly always been a major happiness trigger for me, it has also helped me get in touch with feelings of sadness, fear, or anxiety. I remember being at day camp and hearing some horrible news about the Vietnam War and feeling really down. I couldn't have been more than seven years old. "Rainy Days and Mondays" by the Carpenters came on the radio and I just sat on the swings allowing myself to feel the music and relate to it. The music had the power to help me process my feelings, and I immediately felt better. Steven Tyler once told me that we all have what he calls "inner musical vibration," and though I had no idea at the time, I feel sure that is what the seven-year-old me was experiencing.

When I was a little older, music saw me through my first real heartbreak. It was the age-old story: Boy likes girl. Girl cheats on boy with his best friend. Your classic high school drama. I was miserable, sad, and angry, but I would not allow myself to feel it. I was not about to shed any tears, so I just blocked it all out.

One day, I found myself sitting at the top of my driveway in Woodbourne, New York, when "Just Once" by Quincy Jones came on the radio. Hearing that song made the pain of being cheated on and dumped wash over me like a tidal wave, and I finally allowed myself to lose it. I cried uncontrollably. It was cathartic. When it was over, I felt better and was able to let it go and move on.

Even then, though it wasn't clear how, I knew I would someday use the power of music to help people. I had no idea that years later, I would be channeling this energy into battling addiction.

EARLY DRUG USE

My descent into the abyss of drug addiction started at age eleven. One of my counselors at day camp took out a pipe with a bowl of weed and started passing it around to all the kids. It was an experience I will never forget. Picture me: an innocent, geeky little eleven-year-old. This older kid was passing me drugs. I gave him a look that said, "What am I supposed to do with this?"

In his heavy Brooklyn accent he said, "What? You never partied before?" I may or may not have said no, but I did take a hit. I didn't know how to inhale, so I didn't get high, but I remember the feeling of wanting to be included, not wanting to be left out. The peer pressure, that overused cliché, was stronger than my will to resist. From my mid-teens to early twenties, I was smoking weed and getting high every day.

What began with pot soon escalated into experimentation with other drugs, from hallucinogens to alcohol to cocaine. Pills were never really my thing. Quaaludes, which had once been a huge part of the scene, were on the way out, so I missed that party. My affair with hard drugs eventually took over my life.

I got to the point where I lived to use and used to live. I went from being a good kid who ate dinner with his family every Sunday night to living on the street, depressed, with no family, no friends, no money, and no purpose. I was contemplating suicide.

HITTING BOTTOM

During my teens, I fell deeper down the rabbit hole of drug use. At that age, I was emotionally immature and devoid of any coping skills. By the time I hit bottom, I had become isolated. I was no longer hanging out in clubs or at friends' houses. I was literally in a bathroom or in a closet somewhere getting high. I was totally paranoid, peeking out from under the window shades, imagining I was under surveillance. I was faced with a choice between some pretty severe consequences or treatment. Music was the only beacon of light in my life at that point, my only companion, my only hope.

Once my parents cut me off, treatment centers became my new family. I was in and out of ten different treatment centers in the first two years of my attempt at recovery. I spent time experiencing every type of treatment approach there is.

MY PROFESSIONAL START

My first exposure to working with clients was at Veritas, a therapeutic community in upstate New York modeled after Synanon. Developed in California in the 1960s as an alternative to prison, Synanon was a two-year treatment facility that was more like a military boot camp.

I first came to Veritas as a client, and back then, once you were a client, you could work your way up and eventually be hired from within. One day, a counselor didn't show up for work, so I was asked to fill in and run the group. It went so well they actually ended up putting me through school, which is how I officially got my professional start.

The therapeutic community approach was designed to be extremely confrontational. The premise assumed that if you could sit in a chair for sixteen hours straight without even brushing your teeth, the next time you had the urge to shoot up, you could resist it with willpower. There was no anchor or indicator to rely on. It was all about self-discipline, which was like harshly telling an addict to just to get over it. Would you believe that after you completed the program, they gave you drinking privileges? That's how deeply they misunderstood the addicted personality.

PUSHING MEDS TO CURE ADDICTION

From there, I worked in detoxes and psych hospitals, and it was always the same. It was all about pushing meds. Once clients in detox were able to talk, they had to leave. There was no therapy to speak of. It was a simple routine: take a pill, go back to bed for four hours, then take another pill. Lather, rinse, repeat.

The psych hospitals were focused more on labeling addiction as mental illness. I wanted to say to clients, "No dude, you're not crazy. You're just an addict." There is no question that an addict who stops using is going to be depressed, and the medical profession will be there with the drugs to treat the depression. That is neither an accurate nor complete diagnosis.

You name a type of facility and I worked there, including what I call the Gucci treatment programs that attract all the celebrities and are more about pampering than recovery. As a therapist at one of those, I was only helping people who had money. I thought, "This is not enough. I want to be able to help everybody." Also, more often than not, the indoor gym, tennis courts, and lobster lunches combined with the requisite psychobabble creates a false sense of success that does not translate to the world outside.

As I was dealing with the frustration of all these treatments that were not working, I was motivated to come up with a solution.

COURT LIAISON AND DRUG COURT

A phone call from jail became a turning point in my career. One of my clients had been arrested. He called from the county lockup and said, "Hey, Paul. Can you come to court for me next Tuesday and let the judge know that when I don't take my meds I run around naked?" (or whatever antisocial behavior he was being charged with).

I was happy to help. I didn't think he belonged in jail. After I testified on his behalf, one of the public defenders approached me with an idea.

He said, "I saw what you did in court. I saw how you got your client treatment instead of jail time. My public defenders don't have time to play social worker. Would you be willing to contract with us to be our court liaison?"

Having no real idea what was in store, I said, "Sure!"

That one court appearance morphed into a new career as a successful court liaison. The program was working so well that a group of us came up with the idea to create a mental health and drug court to specifically deal with alcohol- and drug-related offenders. At that time, 85 percent of drug and alcohol offenders would wind up in jail instead of treatment. Jail would not solve their problems. There had to be a better solution.

Of course, for some offenders, prison is unavoidable. The majority, however, would be better off in a treatment facility. So I helped create the Mental Health and Drug Court of Broward County, Florida. It was eventually used as a model for the rest of the country.

THE POWER OF MUSICAL CONNECTION

One day, as the court liaison, I was called upon to pick up two clients from jail. One of them was a skinhead with a swastika tattoo on his arm. He had just finished an eight-year stint in prison. I thought, "Oh my gosh, I'm glad I'm not alone with this guy."

As we were headed back to the halfway house, the Marshall Tucker Band song "Can't You See" came on the car radio. Looking in the rearview mirror at the skinhead, I could see he had tears in his eyes.

I asked, "Hey, you all right?"

He said, "This was one of my favorite songs before I went to prison. It reminds me of my wife, who died while I was in prison, and I never got to say goodbye."

Then he just broke down. You could tell that he had been holding that in for years. You can't exactly show emotions when you're in prison, or as part of the Aryan Nation.

At that moment a realization hit me. I could have spent hours with this guy trying to get him to open up, and chances are, he never would have said a word about his pain and loss. But the music accomplished that task in thirty seconds. It was such a powerful moment. I didn't have a fully fleshed out concept yet, but I knew I was on to something and music was going to be a key part of it.

REHAB CONSULTANT

Around that same time, I started my own consulting firm to help people open drug and alcohol rehabilitation centers, in addition to working as the court liaison. I became very familiar with health care law, licensures and regulations, marketing practices and procedures, as well as zoning restrictions for rehab facilities. Over the next twenty-plus years as a consultant, I helped open dozens of treatment centers in South Florida. I became a substantial resource and was able to help everyone, regardless of clinical, medical, legal, or financial issues. It was very rewarding.

I was also working as the court liaison and doing my best to put clients—like the skinhead—into treatment instead of a jail cell. But once they got to treatment, it was the same old story. It was all psychobabble and the typical defensive treatment model. "You better not take drugs, or else." Even though they had an opportunity to avoid prison and get some real help, they weren't getting it. They would relapse, violate their probation, and boom, they would be facing serious jail time. In spite of my efforts, the cycle of destruction continued.

On top of that, I was being approached by some seriously shady characters who wanted me to help them open treatment facilities. Most of them were only in it for the money, and that bothered me. It was disheartening. I kept thinking, "Since 97 percent of all rehab clients relapse, it's pretty clear we have a real handle on what is not working." I knew there had to be a better way. A way to heal the spirit and give clients a real chance at a true and lasting recovery.

THE FOUNDERS GET TOGETHER

I knew I wanted to explore the power of music in treating addiction. But to really make it happen, I would have to form a new type of rehab center. And it would take partners, legal expertise, and finance. Most important, I wanted to make sure whomever I partnered with was honest, trustworthy, and above all, in it for the right reasons.

I had known Marshall Geisser for more than twenty years. He was a talented lawyer and a former public defender, often representing defendants in the drug courts of Broward County. That's how we got to know each other. Eventually, Marshall went into private practice. I admired him because he would always look out for his clients first, and he'd make every decision in their best interests, even if it cost him money.

Marshall and I would have lunch every couple of months, and we'd talk about our lives and families. Rarely would we talk about business—until one day, Marshall asked me why I had helped so many other people start rehab facilities but never started one of my own. It was a fair question. On a few occasions, I had attempted to collaborate with some people, but it never worked out, usually because our personalities and motivations for being in the business didn't fit well together.

But at this time in my life, it felt different. It felt like this musical treatment concept was a mission from God that I was meant to make into a reality. I still wanted to be sure I trusted whomever I worked with. They had to be in it for the right reasons. Marshall suggested that we should work together, along with his friend Andrew Sossin, to start a rehab center.

I already knew Marshall was trustworthy. I had known him for years by this point. When I met Andrew, he also seemed like a straight shooter, and he had a solid reputation as an honest businessman. We vetted each other for months before we met again. The first question we asked each other at our next meeting was, "Are we in this to make money or save lives?" We all agreed, "We want to help people first. We'll worry about the money later." That was the right answer, and it was kind of the prerequisite for all of us to go forward. I took a leap of faith and told them about my idea for a treatment center based on harnessing the power of music to treat addiction.

LET'S DO THIS

They loved it and said, "We're on board. Let's do this." Our company was born. I was the creator of the concept, as I had experience opening dozens of rehab centers; Marshall was the attorney who was familiar with the regulations and the legal system; and Andrew was the business and finance guy who would be finding investors and securing funding.

Marshall and Andrew handled the business end of things, and I came up with the ideas and formulated the clinical treatment plan. We brought in another partner, Rob Harrison, to run operations. Rob turned out to be a genius at building the business, and he's now spearheading our national expansion.

At first, we called our company Harmony Treatment Center. But none of us really loved the name. It just didn't fit what we were doing. Interestingly, I kept talking about a musician named Richie Supa who is an award-winning singer-songwriter and used to tour with Aerosmith. Richie owned a company called Recovery Unplugged and would be hired to come in and facilitate ninety-minute musical group sessions at detoxes, halfway houses, and treatment centers.

Richie had heard about what we were doing, and he reached out to me. Soon we were talking to Richie because we knew he would be a natural fit for Harmony.

We asked him, "Are you looking for a home?"

And Richie said, "Yeah, I love what you're doing. I'd love to be a part of this."

We offered him a full-time job as our creative director, and he's been the musical center of our program ever since.

Before Richie joined the company, we would put lyrics up on the screen, talk about the lyrics, and then play a recording of a song. Now, with Richie on board, the focus has shifted to emphasize live music. We encourage our clients to create live music. We have recording studios in our facilities. Even clients who have no musical skills can do spoken poetry. If they can turn their words into poetry, we can put a beat to it. Or they can create a rap. We give everyone the opportunity, if they want, to create in our facility.

"YOU GUYS ARE RECOVERY UNPLUGGED!"

One day we had a meeting to brainstorm ideas for a new company name. We were writing all these possible names up on the wall, but nothing jumped out at us.

All of a sudden, someone said, "You know what you guys really are? You guys are Recovery Unplugged!"

We all just kind of sat there for a second, and then I said, "You know, that's right."

Richie, who owned the name Recovery Unplugged, looked at us and said, "You guys can have it."

He just gave it to us because he knew the name was a perfect fit for what we were doing. He didn't ask for anything in return. However, Richie was made a partner in the company because it was the right thing to do.

And that's the way we've always operated. The business was founded on the principle that we would do the right thing, save lives first, and not worry about the money. Every one of our founders, partners, and staff members is on board with this philosophy. And to this day, we have lived that value every day with every client.

ARE YOU OR A LOVED ONE SUFFERING FROM ADDICTION? CONTACT US.

Call us 24/7 at 1-800-55-REHAB (73422)

or visit our website, RecoveryUnplugged.com.

THE MOVEMENT

Our flagship treatment facility is just minutes from the ocean in Fort Lauderdale. It is the hub in a huge wheel of change. Our three locations in Austin, Texas, include a twenty-five-bed residential facility, a fifteen-bed detox center, and a state-of-the-art outpatient facility. We are in the process of opening additional facilities soon in Allendale, Virginia, and Nashville, Tennessee. Our goal is to open a new facility in a different city every year.

Recovery Unplugged is a springboard from which we are impacting the overall climate of drug addiction treatment. As we weave our philosophy into the fabric of the rehab world, our vision is to create Recovery Unplugged centers throughout the country—even the world—while reaching beyond therapeutic boundaries to showcase our musical message on a larger stage.

By expanding our footprint, we are steering the conversation away from pharmaceuticals and raising awareness of the Recovery Unplugged solution. We seek not only to change the concepts of addiction and treatment, but also to shine a light on sobriety, proving to addicts that they don't have to be high to enjoy music and celebrate life.

Whether being asked to participate in the Winter Music Conference in Miami or receiving an invitation to the White House, Recovery Unplugged is striking a chord that is resonating nationally.

WINTER MUSIC CONFERENCE

Founded in 1985, the Winter Music Conference (WMC) is Miami's most prestigious electronic music conference. Participants, including both industry and nonindustry enthusiasts from over seventy countries, converge on Miami Beach to attend over four hundred seminars, panels, workshops, parties, DJ spinoffs, and networking events.

As invitees to the first-ever panel discussion on addiction, our involvement in the WMC signified a radical departure from their typical program. The seminar was educational and informative, and the impact on the audience was awe-inspiring. Many were moved to tears as we attacked the myth that addicts are skid-row bums in dirty trench coats living on the fringe.

One young man expressed the sentiment of the group when he said, "I've been going to all these different classes since I've been here, and all I've been hearing about is how to set up equipment. Now you're finally talking to me about addiction and solutions." He was astounded.

We had audience members seeking us out after the seminar to find out how they could get help for themselves or loved ones. Several came to the facility the following week to see it for themselves.

RECOVERY UNPLUGGED® AT THE WHITE HOUSE

You know you're moving in the right direction when you get a call from the White House. District of Columbia Senator Paul Strauss set up a meeting with Dalen Harris, Associate Director of the Office of National Drug Control Policy, Executive Office of the President. We met in the executive offices of the White House in a room with an enormous conference table, surrounded by pictures of presidents and generals. There was a podium in the room with the presidential seal on it. It was a far cry from Recovery Unplugged's informal environment, and it was pretty clear this was where important decisions were made about the country and the world.

Dalen Harris was sharply dressed in a dark suit. He looked like he was all business. After introducing ourselves, we needed a way to break the ice and establish rapport. I decided to practice what we preach, and I approached him with the universal language.

I said, "Mr. Harris, do you like music?"

He replied, "Yes, I have a thousand songs on my MP3 player."

"Oh really? Where are you from?"

"Staten Island."

"Have you ever heard of the Wu-Tang Clan?"

He looked shocked and said, "Yes, of course. That is where they are from."

Immediately we connected. We started talking music. We started talking lyrics. The ice was broken, and we got down to business. We presented the Recovery Unplugged philosophy, and we strategized about raising awareness of addiction issues and dealing with high recidivism rates.

Thanks to our musical connection, we were able to cut through all the static and really communicate with Dalen Harris. That meeting led to our involvement in the epic UNITE to Face Addiction event.

UNITE to Face Addiction

UNITE to Face Addiction was a major rally and live music event held on October 4, 2015, on the National Mall at the foot of the Washington Monument to raise awareness for addiction and recovery. Performers included Steven Tyler, Sheryl Crow, and Joe Walsh, and featured special greetings from President Obama, Sir Paul McCartney, and Ringo Starr.

UNITE to Face Addiction was conceived to debunk the shame and stigma surrounding drug use and to launch a large-scale attack on the addiction problem. It is similar in scope to the fights against cancer, heart disease, and diabetes. It is dedicated to influencing public policy so the right kind of help becomes available to all addicts, regardless of financial circumstances.

When it was in the planning stages, the event organizers called Richie to see if he could get Steven Tyler to take part. Richie asked, Steven accepted, and we all joined Steven, Joe Walsh, Sheryl Crow, and about twenty well-known musicians onstage. It was an honor to be included, and it was further validation of the legitimacy of our voice.

FACE THE MUSIC FOUNDATION

One of the heartbreaks of the drug and alcohol rehabilitation business is having to turn away clients in need who have neither the money nor insurance to cover the cost. Over the years, we've learned to be creative and send clients to halfway houses and outpatient programs. It's not enough. If they can't pay the bill for residential treatment, they are not getting the help they need. We appealed to some of Florida legislators in Tallahassee but with no results. Marching on Washington and lobbying before Congress was also fruitless.

We wanted to find a way to take money and insurance out of the equation and base care solely on need.

It occurred to us that we were in a unique position to have access to a fairly large contingent of talented, even legendary musicians. We began to see the possibility of putting on concerts to raise money through corporate sponsorships, donations, and a cover charge. That money could be used to give addicts free or assisted access to a network of providers, including Recovery Unplugged. With the help of a group of dedicated professionals, the Face the Music Foundation was born.

Our first event attracted five hundred people and raised over fifty thousand dollars. We used that money to underwrite clients and pay for everything, including basic needs like buying a bicycle for transportation or dental work. The foundation continues to grow and hopefully will become a go-to resource for addicts in need of financial assistance to pay for rehab.

The musical group Zeds Dead gave a portion of the proceeds from their recent tour to Face the Music, and we are hoping to encourage other donations from the music world. The feedback and support so far has been very encouraging. We anticipate many more concerts and live events to continue providing financial assistance to clients who can't afford treatment.

MUSICARES

MusiCares is the Grammy-sponsored foundation that provides support and assistance to recording artists and others associated with the music industry who are struggling with addiction. Recovery Unplugged and the Face the Music Foundation have developed a close relationship with MusiCares. They have total confidence in our concept and are always referring clients to us.

We've had many well-known rock 'n' roll superstars find

their way to recovery through our program. They always know their anonymity will be protected. We also collaborate with MusiCares to stage fundraisers and live events.

CHANGING THE RECOVERY WORLD

We are trying to change the recovery world one client at a time, and maybe even one song at a time. What better way to draw attention to the vital role that rehab and recovery play in our society than with a song? After meeting with one of the creators of the 1985 hit song "We Are the World," Ken Kragen, we were inspired to craft a global anthem to unite the world in the crusade for recovery.

Steven Tyler is the one who lit the fire when he said, "Dude, I've been there and done that. There's nothing else for me to do except give back and help people who are living the nightmare I've lived."

Our goal is to reach out to artists who are in long-term recovery and put together an event reminiscent of Live Aid. We want to create a signature recovery anthem that will become as identifiable as "We Are the World."

Imagine including hip-hop artists who are notorious for glamorizing drugs and misogyny in their music. Those same performers, many of whom are actually in recovery, could rock the recovery world, sending a strong positive message instead of a negative one. We are laying the groundwork as more and more recovering celebrities are dropping by Recovery Unplugged to lend their support and perform for our clients.

As mentioned earlier, Kevin Martin from Candlebox stopped by to perform. He has a lot of experience with addiction himself, and with so many friends like Kurt Cobain overdosing, he shared his gratitude for being alive.

Flo Rida, a multiple Grammy Award-winning rapper, visited Recovery Unplugged and shared his struggles growing up on the streets of Miami. He told our clients his inspirational story about taking calculated risks and never giving up. He's been very supportive of getting our message out.

We know there are some who will criticize this big idea and call us dreamers. They did the same thing when we first launched Recovery Unplugged. And now we've opened our third and fourth facilities. Our motto has always been, "Dream big or go home." And when it comes to America's catastrophic addiction epidemic, no dream is too big.

CHANGE IS GONNA COME

Sam Cooke wrote and recorded the song "A Change Is Gonna Come" in 1964 as a theme song for the Civil Rights Movement. Its timeless message is easily applied to the discrimination and humiliation attached to addiction. We live in a world where addiction is the only disease that people are told they don't have.

Instead of getting appropriate, effective treatment, addicts are chastised and admonished to stop making bad choices. Our mission is to educate the public and make this a discussion that is more humane and compassionate, and less morally judgmental. It is only then that change is gonna come in terms of not only how we help addicts, but how society views them.

Before Recovery Unplugged, the typical treatment path was, like the AC/DC song, a "Highway to Hell." Today our treatment facilities are using music as never before, to communicate with the soul and break the cycle of addiction.

INTRODUCING RICHIE'S LATEST ALBUM, *ENEMY*

We are so lucky to have Richie as part of the Recovery Unplugged team, and we're excited about his new album *Enemy*, the first album totally dedicated to recovery. Truthful, unfiltered, and both poignant and humorous, its lyrics are written straight from Richie's heart in a language that touches addicts where they live. It traces the gamut of emotions in the struggle to recover.

The response from the music industry has been incredible, with descriptions like "brilliant" and "epic." We are hoping to see it nominated for a Grammy in a newly created category of inspirational music. Even more importantly, it will reinforce our movement and become an integral and powerful part of our recovery repertoire.

In terms of publicity, press, and name recognition, Richie has definitely been the face of the facility. He's opened a lot of doors for us. But our concept is universal, and its success does not hinge on any one individual. As our client exit interviews indicate, Richie is definitely beloved, but our overall philosophy and our staff are getting equally rave reviews.

Together we gave birth to a concept that stands on its own, where no one person is more important than the music. Regardless of who is at the helm of Recovery Unplugged, we have much work to do and thousands of people to help get clean.

HOPE FOR THE FUTURE OF RECOVERY

Watching Richie record the highly acclaimed *Enemy* album and experiencing the power of his lyrics and music, we realize how far we have come in our journey. Yes, the "enemy" is unrelenting, but armed with an unlimited musical arsenal, we are filled with hope for the future.

Witnessing the metamorphoses of Recovery Unplugged clients has given us renewed inspiration. Seeing them turn tragedy into triumph lets us know that we are making a concrete difference and effecting real change in the system.

Every day, music is giving Recovery Unplugged clients a new perspective, changing the way they view themselves, and making the world of recovery a kinder, gentler place. We are proving with 100 percent certainty that music is the key to battling addiction. Music is a positive recovery trigger that can anchor, motivate, and inspire addicts to stay clean.

But don't take our word for it. We invite anyone reading this book to call our bluff. We welcome the challenge. Test the power of music for yourself. Choose lyrics that are meaningful to you. Play songs that will improve your mood. Whether you are an addict or not, test the theory on yourself.

YOU MADE IT TO THE END

At the beginning of this book we asked you to just read the first chapter. Well, it appears you read Chapter 1...and then kept reading. We're glad you did. I hope you now have a better perspective on addiction, treatment, the overdose epidemic, the history of rehab, and the power of music to effect great change in all of us.

I now ask readers of this book to take a simple challenge. It will show and prove how music can be a powerful tool in your life, the same powerful tool that recovering addicts need. Music has the ability to change your mood, to bring you back in time, to help you heal from the past, to motivate you to move forward, and to help you stay present. Most importantly, music has the ability to trigger an association that will become the catalyst for recovery.

Here is the challenge: Think of a special time from your past when a favorite song was playing. If you need help thinking of one, maybe you could call a parent, sibling, significant other, best friend, or even look at old videos of a wedding or special event. Once that song is found, go into a room and listen to it. Or listen to it with that family member or friend who was there with you at the event. See where the song takes you. See if it brings you back to the feelings you had. See if it can be used as a catalyst to reinforce whatever mood or serenity you're looking for.

I think you will see the power that a song has to bring you back to a particular place and remind you of how you felt at that time. This challenge is a small example of how a song can hold so much power. I think it will help reinforce what I've been talking about in this book.

CONTACT US

If you are struggling with addiction, or you have a family member who is, there is action you can take. In fact, there is action you *must* take. Please visit our website to learn more about the Recovery Unplugged program and how it can help. Or better yet, pick up the phone and call us. Do it now. We're waiting for your call, and we are ready to help. You can call twenty-four hours a day, seven days a week.

The number is 1-800-55-REHAB (73422).

Let us put the power of music to work for you or your loved one. If you make that call, I promise you, just like the Allman Brothers sang, "Your Soul Will Shine."

ABOUT THE AUTHOR

PAUL PELLINGER is the Chief Strategy Officer of Recovery Unplugged® nationally. For more than 25 years, he has been helping those who struggle with addiction. With Recovery Unplugged® he's found a way to use music to communicate with the soul, where a long-lasting change happens.

.

29937977R00098

Made in the USA
Columbia, SC
29 October 2018